Health and Safety
Commission

**Approved Code
of Practice**

The protection o... g
radiation arisi... y
...85

London: Her Majesty's Stationery Office

© *Crown copyright 1985*
First published 1985
Second impression 1986

Any enquiries regarding this publication should be addressed to the
Health and Safety Executive at any area office or the Public Enquiry Point,
St Hugh's House, Stanley Precinct, Bootle, Merseyside L20 3QY
tel 051-951 4381.

ISBN 0 11 883838 5

Preface

Radiation protection is concerned with the protection of people both individually and in general against detrimental effects of exposure to radiation, while still allowing necessary activities from which radiation exposure might arise. The effects of radiation exposure can be of two types. On the one hand there is the type of effect (called stochastic) for which the probability of occurrence is a function of the dose received. At the dose range involved in radiation protection of workers and those affected by work activities hereditary effects and carcinogenesis are regarded as being of this type. On the other hand there is a type of effect (called non-stochastic) of which the severity depends on the dose received, but for which there is no effect below a certain threshold. Cataracts and skin ulcerations are examples of this type.

In order to minimise both of these effects the primary aim of the Regulations and this Code of Practice is to introduce conditions whereby doses of ionising radiation can be maintained at an acceptable level considerably below the threshold value for the latter type of effect and where the probability of occurrence of the former type of effect is extremely low. It should be remembered that by far the largest contribution to population dose is from our natural background, e.g. cosmic radiation, external radiation of terrestrial origin and internal radiation from natural radionuclides in the body; the Regulations are only concerned with ionising radiation arising from a work activity.

The Regulations contain the fundamental requirements needed to control exposure to ionising radiation. Details of acceptable methods of meeting those requirements are given in the supporting Code. In each case compliance with a Regulation may be achieved by a method other than that described in the Code thus allowing account to be taken of the latest practices adopted through advancing knowledge. The guidance in the Code attempts to avoid essentially reproducing the wording of a regulatory provision which is conditioned by the words 'where reasonably practicable' (or similar): in such cases it has seemed sufficient and appropriate simply to specify the action advocated.
In cases where alternative methods of achieving the regulatory objective are described but where one method is preferred the preferred method is recommended, with an acknowledgement that where this method is not reasonably practicable the alternative method described is acceptable.

Radiation protection is based on three general principles:
(a) every practice resulting in an exposure to ionising radiation shall be justified by the advantages it produces;
(b) all exposures shall be kept as low as reasonably achievable;
(c) the sum of doses and committed doses received shall not exceed certain limits.

The basic principle in the Regulations, that all necessary steps shall be taken to reduce, so far as reasonably practicable, the extent to which people are exposed to ionising radiation, reflects principles (a) and (b) and means that it is not sufficient merely to observe dose limits.
Thus, those whose undertakings cause people to be exposed to ionising radiation have a duty to weigh the costs of the possible health detriment from exposure against the costs of reducing or eliminating that exposure (taking into account possible risks to health and safety

arising from alternative methods of carrying out the work), to the extent of questioning whether a particular use of ionising radiation can be justified at all.

Additionally, the Regulations introduce a dose value, set at three-tenths of the annual dose limits for workers aged 18 years or over, at which an investigation should be carried out to ensure that doses are being kept as low as reasonably practicable and to initiate remedial measures if they are not.

In order to incorporate principle (c) the Regulations set limits on the amount of dose to be received in any calendar year by various categories of person: workers, trainees, members of the public, women of reproductive capacity, and impose duties on people not to cause those limits to be exceeded. The dose limits refer to the sum of all radiation absorbed and committed, from both external and internal sources, whether by the whole body or part of the body, arising from work activities.

In order to facilitate the control of doses to people, the Regulations require controlled and supervised areas to be identified where certain criteria are met (as described in Schedule 6 to the Regulations) or where there is a likelihood of people receiving doses in excess of three-tenths and one-tenth respectively of the annual dose limit for workers aged 18 years or over. Where a person enters a controlled area he must be designated a classified person unless he enters under a written system of work designed to ensure that he cannot receive a significant dose.

The Regulations require specially appointed doctors to undertake medical surveillance on workers who are to be classified and on classified persons in order to assess their fitness to be classified. A review of medical findings is also catered for. Furthermore there has to be a system for regular assessment of doses received by classified persons and dosimetry services approved by the Health and Safety Executive must be used for this purpose. Individual records must be kept of medical findings and assessed doses. The general requirement to keep doses as low as reasonably practicable is strengthened by the inclusion of a basic requirement to control the source of ionising radiation and by subsequent specific requirements to provide appropriate safety devices, warning signals, handling tools, etc, to leak-test radioactive sources, to provide protective equipment and clothing and to test them, to monitor radiation and contamination levels, to store radioactive substances safely, to design, construct and maintain buildings, fittings and equipment so as to minimise contamination, and to make contingency arrangements for dealing with foreseeable but unintended incidents. In addition, undertakings holding large quantities of radioactive substances will need to make a survey of potential hazards and prepare a report, a copy of which should be sent to the Executive.

The Executive needs to be kept aware of those areas where hazards from ionising radiation might and do arise and there are therefore requirements for people to notify when they use ionising radiation, when there is a release or loss of radioactive substances, and when someone has received an excessive dose of radiation. Local investigations of excessive doses will have to be made and reports kept.

It is important that any equipment, device or other article used in connection with ionising radiation affords optimum radiation protection, and there are therefore duties on designers, manufacturers, importers, suppliers, erectors and installers to undertake their work in such a way that the future use of the article can be conducted in such a way as to reduce doses as far as reasonably practicable.

The provision of information on potential hazards and the instruction and training of people involved with ionising radiation are an essential part of radiation protection, and are required in the Regulations. Additionally there are requirements to formulate written local rules covering all radiation protection arrangements and to provide supervision of work involving ionising radiation. This last requirement will normally necessitate the appointment by management of a radiation protection supervisor whose responsibilities should be clearly defined. Above all, however, it is essential that experts in radiation protection are concerned with work activities where there is a likelihood of people receiving significant doses. The Regulations therefore require radiation protection advisers to be appointed wherever expert advice is needed and for appointments to be notified to the Executive. These appointments in no way affect the rights and responsibilities of safety representatives set out in the Safety Representatives and Safety Committees Regulations 1977; safety representatives should be consulted or information made available, as appropriate, on relevant aspects which may include, dosimetry results, investigations of exposure, designation of controlled areas and classified persons and the implications of local rules. It may also be appropriate to involve them, or in certain circumstances other employee representatives, in the local arrangements for such matters as the provision of information, instruction and training, medical surveillance, monitoring and the provision of personal protective equipment, etc.

Special considerations apply to medical exposures. Doses received by patients undergoing diagnosis or treatment involving the use of ionising radiation are not taken into account in determining compliance with dose limits. However, doses received by those patients as a result of other patients' medical exposures are taken into account. In addition, there is a requirement to investigate and notify certain equipment malfunctions and generally ensure that the clinical objectives of diagnosis or treatment are achieved with the minimum of exposure.

Contents

Notice of Approval

By virtue of section 16(1) of the Health and Safety at Work etc. Act 1974 and with the consent of the Secretary of State for Employment the Health and Safety Commission has on 3 September 1985 approved the Code of Practice *The protection of persons against ionising radiation arising from any work activity.*

The Code of Practice is approved for the purpose of providing practical guidance with respect to the Ionising Radiations Regulations 1985.

The Code of Practice comes into effect on 1 October 1985 which is the date when the Ionising Radiations Regulations 1985 come into operation, for the purposes of Regulation 10.

Signed

C JOHNSON

Secretary to the Health and Safety Commission

Introduction

1 This Code of Practice has been drawn up following widespread consultation with interested parties and in particular in consultation with the Health and Safety Commission's technical working party on proposed legislative requirements for radiological protection, consisting of nominees from the Confederation of British Industry and the Trades Union Congress together with independent experts and with representatives of the Health and Safety Executive. The National Radiological Protection Board has also been consulted (as required by section 16(2) of the Health and Safety at Work etc. Act 1974) and its advice has been incorporated in the Code of Practice.

2 The Code has been approved by the Health and Safety Commission with the consent of the Secretary of State under section 16 of the Health and Safety at Work etc. Act 1974 for the purpose of providing practical guidance with respect to the provisions of the Ionising Radiations Regulations 1985 (SI No. 1333), which themselves implement the majority of the provisions of the European Council Directives 80/836 and 84/467 Euratom laying down the basic safety standards for the health protection of the general public and workers against the dangers of ionising radiation. The provisions of the Code represent, in the opinion of the Health and Safety Commission, the most appropriate methods of complying with the regulatory requirements and, in particular, the methods which should be considered to be reasonably practicable when that term appears in the Regulations. The Code applies to all work activities covered by the Regulations but does not give specific guidance on the application of the Regulations to work involving increased exposure to isotopes of radon and their decay products such as occurs in some non-coal mines, for which there is to be a separate, third, part of this Code of Practice which is presently divided into two parts. Part 1 gives general guidance on all the Regulations for which it is currently recognised that such guidance is necessary. Part 2 is divided into sections which relate to specific work activities: it gives practical guidance on Regulation 6 which is additional to the guidance in Part 1 or in some cases is an alternative to that guidance.

3 Although failure to comply with any provision of the Code is not in itself an offence, such a failure may be used in criminal proceedings as evidence that a person has contravened a Regulation to which the provision relates. In such a case, however, it will be open to that person to satisfy the court that he has complied with the Regulation in some other way.

4 Words and expressions which are defined in the Health and Safety at Work etc. Act 1974 or in the Ionising Radiations Regulations 1985 have the same meaning in this Code unless the context requires otherwise. Any reference in this Code to any publication does not imply approval by the Health and Safety Commission of that publication or any part of it as an Approved Code of Practice except to the extent necessary to give effect to this Code.

PART 1

**REGULATION 2
Interpretation**

Radioactive substance

1 The definition of 'radioactive substance' extends to some substances which, although having an activity concentration equal to or less than $100\,\mathrm{Bqg}^{-1}$, may nevertheless present a radiological hazard. Such substances include zircon, baddeleyite and monazite sands, zirconia, and similar rare earth ores, etc. These examples have low activity concentrations but are often involved in dusty processes and may create an internal radiation hazard from inhalation. Equally, there may be an external radiation hazard from bulk storage of such materials. For substances which include the radionuclides thorium 232 or uranium 238, or any nuclides in their particular decay series, activity concentrations of the parent radionuclides exceeding $0.3\,\mathrm{Bqg}^{-1}$ or $1.0\,\mathrm{Bqg}^{-1}$ respectively for dusty operations, and $5\,\mathrm{Bqg}^{-1}$ or $9\,\mathrm{Bqg}^{-1}$ respectively for bulk storage, would bring them within the definition.

2 Another test which may be applied is if the use of a substance would create, because of its radioactivity, the need for a supervised area to be designated because of the provisions of Regulation 8 and Schedule 6 then that substance should be treated as a radioactive substance.

Medical exposure

3 'Suitably qualified' for the purposes of the definition of 'medical exposure' would be:

(a) in relation to the person clinically directing a medical exposure, a person who has received a qualification in the appropriate branch of the healing arts and who has received adequate training in the radiological techniques which he is clinically directing; and

(b) in relation to the person physically directing that medical exposure, a person who has sufficient knowledge and experience to carry out the exposure in such a way as to achieve the desired result.

**REGULATION 3
Application to the
short-lived daughters
of radon 222**

4 Regulation 3 recognises that certain of the Regulations are not applicable where the work with ionising radiation exposes persons only to the short-lived daughters of radon 222 because the parent radionuclide is a naturally occurring gas. However, the Regulations apply in full to any other work with ionising radiation that may take place in the same area, e.g. a radiation generator used in a place where there is also exposure to radon 222, also where radium or uranium sources are used which give rise to radon 222.

**REGULATION 5
Notification of
certain work with
ionising radiation**

Peripatetic work

5 For peripatetic work, notification of each occasion when work with ionising radiation is undertaken will only be necessary if the Executive has previously invoked the provisions of paragraph (4) of the Regulation.

Form of notification

6 A form which specifies the particulars required and which may be used for notification to the Executive, is reproduced as Appendix 1 to this Code. Where an alternative method of notification is used it should be in writing and contain the particulars listed in Schedule 4 to the Regulations.

Material change

7 A material change will need to be notified to the Executive if the work which is undertaken changes to an extent that would affect the detailed particulars in Schedule 4 of the Regulations previously notified under Regulation 5(2).

REGULATION 6
Restriction of exposure

Steps for dose restriction

8 The determination of what steps would be sufficient to restrict exposure so far as reasonably practicable will be a matter of judgement in any particular set of circumstances. It is important to consider whether a procedure could be carried out as effectively and more safely by some other method.

9 If a choice has to be made between restricting doses to individuals and restricting doses to groups of persons then priority should be given to keeping individual doses as far below dose limits as reasonably practicable. Dose sharing amongst those who normally carry out that work might further reduce individual doses but this should not be used as a primary means of complying with dose limits. In such cases priority should be given to changing the methods of work, improving engineering controls and adopting any other means of restricting exposure so as not to increase significantly the collective dose.

10 Whilst the dose limit for an employee who does not normally work with ionising radiation is the same as that for one who does, it is unlikely that all necessary steps will have been taken to restrict his exposure if the dose received by such an employee exceeds or approaches any of the dose limits specified for 'any other persons' in Schedule 1 to the Regulations, i.e. one-tenth of the adult employee dose limit.

11 Paragraph 171 of this Code deals with investigations which have to be carried out when the whole body dose received by an employee exceeds 15 mSv in a calendar year.

Engineering controls and design features

12 Regulation 6 requires that, first and foremost in any work with ionising radiation, action should be taken to implement the physical safeguards specified in Regulation 6(2), before the other controls in Regulation 6(3) are applied.

13 Engineering controls should almost invariably be provided to reduce exposure to persons from external radiation. These may comprise a combination of local shielding, distance, or primary shielding. When shielding is provided the aim should be to achieve the lowest instantaneous dose rate outside the shielding that is reasonably practicable. In most cases this should be below $7.5\,\mu Svh^{-1}$. Where dose rates above this exist additional controls may be required, e.g. designation of controlled areas.

14 Priority should be given to the containment of radioactive substances as a means of preventing dispersal or contamination rather than by applying ventilation. Where such containment alone is not sufficient to give the required protection, ventilation should be provided. In many cases both containment and ventilation will need to be provided.

15 Ventilation when it is provided should be applied at the likely points of origin of the dispersion of the radioactive substances. Any equipment associated with a ventilation system, including ducting, fan assemblies, filtration units, etc, should be so designed and constructed as to facilitate maintenance, cleaning and decontamination.

16 When a building, room or other enclosure is built or modified it should incorporate design features which have been pre-planned and constructed in such a way that has regard to the work being undertaken and extent of contamination which could result from it. Means of safe access, ease of cleaning and decontamination, provisions for decommissioning or dismantling, are some of the considerations which should be applied in determining whether all that is reasonably practicable has been achieved. Advice on provisions relating to washing and changing facilities in places where contamination is likely to arise is given under paras 133 to 136 of this Code.

17 There is no level of contamination specified as acceptable. The aim should be to achieve the lowest level that meets the requirements of Regulation 6(2). If a spillage or dispersion occurs during normal work then this should be cleaned up without delay. Contamination should not be accepted and used as a basis for designating a controlled or supervised area. One exception to this procedure would be where the collective dose from cleaning up would exceed the collective dose for leaving it alone, e.g. short-lived radionuclides may sometimes be left to decay rather than cleaning them up. Nevertheless there may be circumstances in practice where it is necessary to clean up the area albeit at the expense of higher collective doses: such circumstances might include areas to which other people have access, when restriction of exposure to those persons may be paramount or when the material presents another, more imminent, risk to health and safety. A radiation protection adviser may make use of standard tables of derived limits to help indicate whether a particular level of surface contamination needs further reduction or whether an article may be moved out of a controlled area without further decontamination. However, care should be exercised in making comparisons between the tables and actual measurements as the individual circumstances may differ from the model used to arrive at the levels in the tables. Unless controls are exercised to prevent items leaving the site without additional contamination checks, the remaining levels of contamination should be reduced below the levels allowed for transport away from the site.

Safety features and warning devices

18 Safety features and warning devices should be provided whenever they are likely to contribute either directly or indirectly to the restriction of exposure.

19 Safety features and warning devices include the following:

(a) means of initiating and terminating the output from a radiation generator and controlling the output from a radioactive substance;

(b) devices that under certain specified conditions prevent the output from a radiation generator or from a radioactive substance, e.g. interlocking arrangements which are designed in such a way that if they fail to operate no emission or exposure can occur;

(c) devices that under certain specified conditions bring about the termination of the output from a radiation generator or from a radioactive substance, e.g. interlocking arrangements which are designed in such a way that if they fail to operate any emission or exposure is immediately terminated and cannot be reinitiated without resetting the device;

(d) devices that prevent access to certain areas whilst either a radiation generator is emitting ionising radiation or there is exposure to ionising radiation from a radioactive substance in a source container;

(e) 'search and lock-up' systems designed so that areas in which radiation generators are about to be energised to emit ionising radiation or exposure to radiation from a source is about to occur are checked to ensure that no person is present. The check should be confirmed by the operation of 'search buttons' within a predetermined time before the area is closed and irradiation begins; these devices would only be expected in places where very intense sources are used, such as accelerators or sterilisation plants;

(f) automatic or manually operated audible, visible or illuminated warning signals designed to convey specific warnings to persons in the vicinity of installations or equipment that can produce ionising radiation;

(g) emergency devices, such as 'off buttons' placed in appropriate locations, whereby persons may prevent, or quickly interrupt, the emission of ionising radiation from machines or exposure to radiation from radioactive sources;

(h) labels, notices, etc, that convey specific, clear and unambiguous information to persons in the vicinity of installations or equipment that can produce ionising radiation (see also the Safety Signs Regulations 1980 (SI 1980 No. 1471) and British Standards BS 3510: 1968 and BS 5378: 1980);

(i) radiation detectors that are used to locate or to confirm the location of sources or beams of ionising radiation or to operate radiation alarms;

(j) devices, such as stops, that prevent the useful beam from a source of ionising radiation being aligned in certain directions or collimators that limit the spread of such a beam; and

(k) devices to detect fire or explosion.

This list is not intended to be exhaustive.

20 In many cases combinations of safety features and/or combinations of warning devices may be needed to satisfy Regulation 6(2). Specific additional guidance for many applications is given in Part 2 of this Code.

Systems of work

21 Whenever work with ionising radiation is undertaken systems of work, i.e. detailed working arrangements, should be adopted which ensure that the provisions of Regulation 6(1) and (2) are fulfilled. In circumstances where a person working with ionising radiations could, under normal or abnormal conditions, receive an overexposure in a relatively short period of time such as several minutes or less, these detailed arrangements may require formalising to an extent which may involve the issue of a certificate of entry specifying the detailed working arrangement for that entry. These formalised systems are frequently known as 'permit-to-work systems'.

NOTE   Written systems of work for entry of non-classified persons into controlled areas, as required by Regulation 8(6), are dealt with in paragraphs 49 to 51.

Personal protective equipment

22 Personal protective equipment should be of a type which protects the person against the hazards likely to be encountered. Information, instruction and training in its use should be in conformity with Regulation 12.

23 After use, personal protective equipment should be cleaned (or disposed of) if during its use it has become contaminated.

24 The term 'adequate' with respect to personal protective equipment refers to the ability of the equipment to protect the wearer. Where contamination is present, the design and material of the equipment may also contribute to protecting other people such as laundry workers, people working in changing areas, etc. 'Suitable' refers to the correct matching of the equipment to the job and the person. To be considered adequate and suitable personal protective equipment should be correctly selected and used.

25 In selecting and using respiratory protective equipment reference should be made to British Standard BS 4275: 1974 and attention should be paid to:

(a) the nature of the radioactive substance and the nature and degree of exposure;

(b) the face fit for the individual who has to wear it;

(c) wearability and comfort;

(d) the length of time the equipment is to be worn;

(e) any limitations on its performance stated either by the manufacturer, or in any relevant approved standard, or in a certificate of type approval from the Executive.

26 As a means of restricting exposure to ionising radiations from radioactive substances entering the body in contaminated areas:

(a) facilities should be provided in non-contaminated areas for the activities prohibited under Regulation 6(6);

(b) arrangements should be made to ensure that persons who have any cuts or abrasions do not enter controlled areas unless those cuts or abrasions are effectively covered;

(c) disposable handkerchieves should be provided;

(d) arrangements should be made to prevent direct ingestion from contaminated articles or from radioactive substances; and

(e) nursing mothers should not be employed in work involving a high risk of radioactive contamination; special supervision and control should be provided to minimise bodily radioactive contamination.

27 Further restriction of exposure by the provision of a particular form of personal protective equipment may be considered to be inappropriate, albeit reasonably practicable, when its use would render the wearer liable to other forms of risk greater than that arising from the ionising radiation; it may be more appropriate in these circumstances to use another type, or even none at all. Examples of where the balance of choice could be affected include:

(a) where work is done in confined spaces with breathing apparatus and the bulkiness of self-contained breathing apparatus could lead the wearer to become trapped, then airline breathing apparatus may be appropriate; or

(b) where wearing gloves in close proximity to revolving parts could present considerable risk to the wearer. This would not alleviate the requirement to provide overalls and overshoes, etc, if these were necessary, merely because gloves were inappropriate.

Further provisions relating to restriction of exposure

28 More specific provisions for certain processes are set out in Part 2 of this Code. These relate to the following uses of ionising radiation:

Section 1   Diagnostic radiology using X-ray equipment for medical exposures and in veterinary practice
Section 2   Radiation beam therapy
Section 3   Diagnostic use of radioactive sources
Section 4   Radioactive substances used in or on the body
Section 5   X-ray baggage and postal inspection systems
Section 6   Non-medical radiography and irradiation (including research)
Section 7   Site radiography
Section 8   Use of gauging and detection devices and sources of incidental ionising radiation
Section 9   X-ray optics.

REGULATION 7
Dose limits

Committed dose

29 The words 'committed dose equivalent' refer to the dose equivalent accruing over the period of 50 years following the intake of radioactive material. Once the committed dose or committed effective dose equivalent has been assessed for a particular dosimetric period it is attributed to that period for the purpose of compliance with the dose limits. Thus the only effective method of controlling and limiting the committed dose quantity is by controlling and limiting the intake.

Doses to a foetus

30 Parts IV and V of Schedule 1 to the Regulations give additional limits intended to control doses to a foetus, but do not take specific account of committed dose equivalent to the foetus. Because of this special care should be taken to restrict intake when a pregnant woman is exposed to a dispersible radioactive substance.

Averaging

31 Doses to organs and tissues should normally be averaged over their volume, with the exception of skin which is specifically covered in Part II of Schedule 1 to the Regulations. In assessing dose equivalent to any part of the body from narrow beams of external radiation, or from very small spots of contamination, it would be inappropriate to average the dose over an area of more than 1 cm² for the purpose of comparison with dose limits, unless the radiation protection adviser or approved dosimetry service has sound evidence to average over a larger area.

32 It should be noted that averaging activity for the purpose of dose assessment under Regulation 13 should be made over an appropriate area which should not exceed 100 cm². When monitoring is carried out under Regulations 6 or 24, to ensure that contamination is not being transferred out of the area or for the purpose of monitoring the body for surface contamination, then the activity should be averaged over an area which does not exceed 300 cm².

Compliance with dose limits

33 In general, external radiation doses are assessed from measurements of doses under some tissue equivalent material. Typically, for weakly penetrating radiation,

measurements under the equivalent of 0.07 mm of tissue would be used to represent the dose equivalent to the skin. For strongly penetrating radiation the equivalent of 10 mm of tissue would be used as a basis for assessing effective dose equivalent.

34 However, correlation between what is measured and the interpretation of the dose received for all the relevant dose limits in Schedule 1 to the Regulations is normally dealt with by an approved dosimetry service. Because the approved dosimetry service has the expertise in these matters, operational quantities relating to dose assessments are not further discussed in this Code.

35 For convenience, the measurements made under specified thicknesses of material may be given special names and definitions, and regarded as physical quantities. Recommendations about such names, and on how measurements of these special quantities relate to dose equivalent quantities, are published from time to time by the International Commission on Radiation Units and Measurements (ICRU) and the ICRP. In the United Kingdom, the British Committee on Radiation Units and Measurements (BCRU) generally follows these recommendations, and may also publish supplementary recommendations or guidance.

36 For the case of exposure to internal radiation following the intake of radioactive substances, the dose limits on committed effective dose equivalent, or committed dose equivalent, may be deemed to be complied with if the intakes, assessed by an approved dosimetry service, do not exceed the relevant annual limit on intake (see Annex III of European Council Directive 80/836 Euratom (as amended by Directive 84/467 Euratom) and ICRP Publication 30).

37 In the case of exposure to external and internal radiation, compliance with the dose limit requirements may be demonstrated on the basis of a combination of dose equivalent and intake (see Annex II of European Council Directive 80/836 Euratom). Technical details of doing this will be known by approved dosimetry services; they will also provide dosemeters suitable for measuring the appropriate dose quantities, will advise on wearing positions and will make the necessary assessments of intakes of radioactive substances.

REGULATION 8
Designation of controlled and supervised areas

Regulation 8(1)

38 Places which cannot physically be entered do not need to be designated in relation to Schedule 6 to the Regulations.

39 Generally there will be no need to designate places which can be entered and which have effective engineering controls that prevent any person from being exposed to an instantaneous dose rate exceeding 7.5 μSvh^{-1}. In such cases any opening should be provided with electrical or mechanical interlocking devices designed to fail to safety. However, if persons enter in order to carry out maintenance, e.g. to change a sealed source, then designation may nevertheless be required.

40 Any area designated as controlled or supervised will remain as such for most of the time. Where the periods during which work with ionising radiation takes place are clearly defined, follow a regular pattern or are only intermittent, the employer may wish to de-designate on a regular basis. This may be done provided that:

(a) the radiation generator is isolated from the power supply or the radioactive substances are removed or otherwise made safe; and

(b) any notices, warnings and the text of the local rules reflect which set of conditions regarding designation exist at any moment in time.

41 The matter to take into account when considering designation of controlled and supervised areas during the movement of radioactive substances is the effect in relation to persons. In general the person accompanying the moving source should be regarded as being in a potential controlled or supervised area, but bystanders are not likely to be in that situation. Under normal conditions of transport it is unlikely that a controlled area would exist outside the edges of a conveyance or package if the radioactive substance is packaged in accordance with the current requirements of the International Atomic Energy Agency (IAEA) in relation to the safe transport of radioactive materials.

Regulation 8(3)

42 The conditions in Schedule 6 requiring the designation of a controlled or supervised area may or may not exist throughout the normal physical boundaries of the work area. If it is more convenient to use those boundaries, e.g. because of the need to control access, then they may be used. An example would be a room in which small radioactive sources are used, where for convenience the employer has decided that the existing walls and doors should form the boundary of the area even though dose rates, surface contamination levels, etc, at the proposed boundary were below the criteria levels for designation. Once such an area has been designated it is subject to all the legal requirements applying to such areas. If a controlled or supervised area exists only in part of a room the whole room need not be designated provided that, in the case of a controlled area, the necessary restrictions on access can be applied.

Regulation 8(4)

43 When a situation arises, e.g. as a result of an accident, that would cause a controlled area to exist (but for the operation of Regulation 8(4)) in a place where the employer does not normally have control then, as part of a contingency plan under Regulation 27, he should try to have the access to that area restricted until the situation returns to normal or until the emergency services take over control of it.

Regulation 8(5)

44 For the convenience of the employer, controlled or supervised areas may be described by reference to fixed features such as walls. Where the source of ionising radiation is mobile the area(s) may be described generically, e.g. by reference to distances from the source (and if necessary from any object irradiated by the source).

45 Physical demarcation of all boundaries of controlled areas may not be reasonably practicable in the following examples:

(a) when a radioactive substance being transported is stationary at the side of a road because of breakdown and along the road there is free-flowing traffic. The area would be demarcated on the kerbside but not in a carriageway;

NOTE   It may not be necessary to designate a controlled area outside the conveyance provided the conditions in Schedule 6(3) and (4) are satisfied.

(b) when a controlled area exists in an upper room of a multi-storey building and extends outside a window to which there is no access. The area would only be demarcated inside the building;

(c) when a person has been administered with a radioactive substance as part of a medical exposure and is subsequently located in part of a room where the whole of that room has not been designated, suitable means for delineation in this case would be a description, kept in a convenient place, of the extent of the controlled area around that patient;

(d) the controlled area is caused by mobile X-ray equipment used for medical exposure which is not routinely used in the same place;

(e) the controlled area is caused by dental radiography medical exposures and has been identified in accordance with paragraph 60; or

(f) the controlled area is caused by X-ray equipment used in veterinary radiography and has been identified in accordance with paragraph 62.

In examples (d), (e) and (f) the operator should be able to see any person in the vicinity of the controlled area and quickly de-energise the X-ray equipment from the normal operating position.

46 The method of demarcation should clearly indicate the extent of the controlled area with no room for doubt. The choice of method will be influenced by the means of restricting access chosen by the employer.

47 Warning signs (to the standard of The Safety Signs Regulations 1980 SI No. 1471 and British Standards BS 3510: 1968 and BS 5378: 1980) and cautionary notices should be used to inform those persons who need to be warned of the existence of a controlled area.

48   In determining whether suitable means of restricting access have been provided it is necessary to take into account the nature of the work and the likelihood that the restrictions will ensure that only those persons who are permitted to enter do so. In most cases physical barriers should be provided. Only where the work is of short duration and transient in nature can continuous supervision, which is effective in preventing access by persons, be a substitute for barriers.

Regulation 8(6)

49   When persons, other than classified persons, enter a controlled area then the entry should only be in accordance with a written system of work, whether or not that person himself is entering to work or is a visitor. Persons entering for the purposes of undergoing a medical exposure are not subject to the provision of the written system of work (see Regulation 2(9)).

50   It may be appropriate for an employer to operate a written system of work for his employees in a case where he has used Regulation 8(3) to designate a whole room as a controlled area for convenience of physical demarcation, e.g. where there is only one small area such as a bench or fume cupboard where work with ionising radiations takes place. In this example, if an employer is certain that non-classified persons could not be exposed to more than three-tenths of any relevant dose limit, then the entry of those persons could be by a written system of work. Another example would be to allow a person who is not normally exposed to ionising radiations to enter a controlled area for a limited period in order to carry out his job. This would be particularly relevant to maintenance work, such as to permit a plumber to enter to repair a central heating radiator. In general, doses to persons who enter controlled areas under written systems of work should be assessed (by individual measurement where appropriate) to monitor the effectiveness of the systems of work and to ensure that persons are classified as necessary.

51   Any written system of work should have due regard to Regulation 6 in restricting dose and only exceptionally should a person working under such a system approach the specified dose restrictions in Regulation 8(6).

52   If personal dose assessments are used to verify that the dose restrictions are met under a written system of work they may be carried out either individually or on a representative sample if several persons enter at one time. It may be convenient to use dosemeters issued by the approved dosimetry service which will assess the doses. Alternatively other dosemeters may be issued and the readings taken directly by the employer, providing he has available the necessary expertise.

53   When personal dosemeters are not used for the purposes of Regulation 8(7), other suitable measurements may include keeping a record of the time spent in the controlled area provided that the dose rate or contamination level is known and is fairly constant or is known not to exceed a particular value.

54   All monitoring instruments (except those supplied by an approved dosimetry service) used to demonstrate compliance with Regulation 8(6)(b) should themselves conform to the requirements of Regulation 24. These would include dose rate monitors, TLD readers, pocket audible alarm monitors and quartz fibre electroscopes.

Schedule 6

55   Because certain areas need not be designated under paras 2 and 3 of Schedule 6 the employer is not relieved of the duty to comply with other Regulations. In particular he should ensure that the requirements of Regulations 6 and 20 in relation to the handling and keeping of sources are met.

56   If an employee in the course of working with ionising radiation enters in any day more than one area to which the exceptions in paragraphs 2, 3, 4 and 6 of Schedule 6 apply, the employer should take suitable steps to ensure that that employee does not exceed more than three-tenths of any relevant dose limit unless he is a classified person. Suitable steps would include: determining the dose from a knowledge of the dose rate and the time of exposure, carrying out dosimetry, or providing measures such as shielding.

57 Averaging for the purpose of paragraph 6(a) of Schedule 6 is permitted over any 8-hour working period. Some employers may wish to run samples for shorter periods and then extrapolate them to an 8-hour exposure. In these cases the sampling should be such that it does not underestimate the 8-hour exposure level. Samples taken over periods longer than 8 hours in order to obtain better accuracy should encompass only typical working periods and should not underestimate exposure in any 8-hour working period.

58 A method of measuring surface contamination levels is given in paragraph 147. Air concentrations and external radiation levels will always need to be taken into account in addition to surface contamination levels when deciding whether an area should be designated. The figures in column 4 of Schedule 2 relate to the ingestion pathway of entry into the body and as such do not relate to fixed contamination. If in any particular set of circumstances it is decided that contamination is fixed then if the circumstances change, a review should be undertaken. Examples would be: where a floor has been contaminated and the process changes such that the floor is abraded or where a benchtop is cleaned with a different solvent (see also paragraph 17).

59 The fact that there is less radioactive substance in an area than the quantity specified in columns 3, 4 or 5 of Schedule 2 does not relieve the employer of the duty to comply with any other requirements of the Regulations (particularly Regulations 6 and 20), even though the area may not need to be designated.

Dental radiography

60 A special case may occur in dental radiography where, if certain specific conditions are met, it is possible to define without further assessment or measurement the extent of the controlled area required in pursuance of Schedule 6, paragraph 1. These conditions are where:

(a) the only source of ionising radiation that may be operated at any one time in any room is a single piece of X-ray equipment, specifically designed either for ordinary dental radiography with intra oral film or for dental panoramic tomography;

(b) the workload of the X-ray equipment does not exceed in any week
  (i) for dental radiography a value of 30 mA minutes, or
  (ii) for dental panoramic tomography a value of 150 mA minutes;

(c) the X-ray equipment is of sound construction and properly maintained; and

(d) the other provisions of Section 1 in Part 2 of this Code are complied with.

The extent of the controlled area when the equipment is operating will then be:

(e) when the X-ray equipment operates at up to 70 kV
  (i) within the primary beam until it has been sufficiently attenuated by distance or by absorption in material,
  (ii) within 1 m of the X-ray tube in any direction, and
  (iii) within 1 m in any direction of the patient under examination; and

(f) when the X-ray equipment operates above 70 kV, the dimensions in (e)(ii) and (iii) should be increased from 1 m to 1.5 m.

When this method is adopted, no supervised area will exist outside the controlled areas defined by (e) and (f) above.

61 The method of identifying controlled areas described in paragraph 60 should not be adopted for other types of work (e.g. cephalometry) except on the advice of a radiation protection adviser.

Veterinary radiography

62 Similarly a special case may occur in veterinary radiography where, if certain specific conditions are met, it is possible to define without further assessment or measurement the extent of the controlled area required in pursuance of paragraph 1 of Schedule 6. These conditions are where:

(a) the only source of ionising radiation that may be operated at any one time in any room is a single piece of X-ray equipment specifically designed for X-ray diagnosis and that equipment is only used with the X-ray beam directed vertically downwards on to the table;

10

(b) the X-ray equipment is fitted with a light beam diaphragm or other device to ensure that the useful beam does not come within 10 cm of the edge of the table;

(c) the table is covered by 1 mm of lead over an area extending not less than 10 cm further in each direction than the largest area of useful beam;

(d) the equipment operates at less than 100 kV; and

(e) the workload of the X-ray equipment does not exceed 4 mA minutes in any week.

The controlled area will then exist between the ceiling and floor in a vertical direction extending 1 m out from each edge of the table.

Other cases of dental and veterinary radiography

63   If any of the specific conditions in paragraphs 60 or 62 are not met then the extent of the controlled area should be determined by reference to the general requirement of Schedule 6, paragraph 1, or where applicable the alternative provisions of Schedule 6, paras 2 and 3.

REGULATION 9
Designation of classified persons

64   In deciding whether a person should be classified it is essential to consider the potential dose in any given set of circumstances; it is not sufficient to rely solely on the individual's avoidance of such a dose in the past. In many cases the reason for designation will be that those individuals work in controlled areas.

65   It should be assumed that persons who work with large sources of ionising radiation (i.e. sources that are capable of exposing a person to the equivalent of an overdose within a few minutes) will need to be classified albeit that calculations on the basis of strict adherence to local rules indicate that doses in excess of three-tenths of any relevant dose limit would not occur.

66   When considering the classification of persons in relation to internally deposited radionuclides three of the factors which should be taken into account are:

(a) the potential for radioactive substances to enter the body;

(b) the likely magnitude of any intake; and

(c) the radiotoxicity of the material being used.

Female employees

67   Where dose rates to the abdomen appear to be such that any female employee might receive more than 13 mSv in any consecutive period of 3 months, then the employer should, in consultation with his radiation protection adviser, make every effort to control exposure so that doses are received more uniformly and do not reach this level. Only if the radiation protection adviser advises that this cannot reasonably be achieved does the question of whether the employee is a woman of reproductive capacity become important in deciding whether she can be exposed in those particular circumstances (see paragraphs 97 and 100(d) dealing with entries in the health record).

REGULATION 10
Appointment of Radiation Protection Advisers and Qualified Persons

68   When an employer appoints a radiation protection adviser (RPA) he should ensure that the person will be available for consultation whenever required. It may not be necessary for the RPA to be present every time that work with ionising radiation takes place. The appointment of qualified persons for the particular purpose of Regulation 24 is dealt with in paragraph 76 but the provisions in paragraphs 70 and 72 will apply.

69   Appointment as a radiation protection adviser may be on a full- or part-time basis depending on circumstances, e.g. a full-time appointment would clearly not be justified in the case of an employer routinely using a gauging device containing a sealed source of ionising radiation. Conversely, a large or complex organisation may need more than one RPA if the range of duties, or scope and complexity of the work with ionising radiation, is such that one person could not reasonably carry out all the functions required.

70 The RPA may be, or become, an employee of the undertaking, alternatively an outside consultant or specialist organisation may be appointed. Where the RPA is a body corporate or partnership, the individual officers of that body should between them have the qualifications and attributes that are required for an individual RPA.

Qualifications, experience, etc, required

71 The qualifications, experience and qualities that a radiation protection adviser should possess include, in so far as they relate to the scope of the advice required of him:

(a) such theoretical training as would ensure that he has the necessary knowledge of the properties of the ionising radiations used in the work undertaken by the employer;

(b) a thorough knowledge of the hazards of the ionising radiations present and how the hazard should be controlled and minimised;

(c) an understanding and detailed knowledge of the working practices used in the establishment to which he is being appointed, as well as a general knowledge of the working practices in other establishments of the same type;

(d) a detailed working knowledge of all statutory provisions, approved codes of practice, other codes of practice, guidance material and other information relevant to his work in giving advice in connection with the work with ionising radiation undertaken by the employer;

(e) the ability to give advice so that the employer can do what is required of him by statute and follow good radiation protection practice;

(f) the calibre and personality to enable him to communicate with the employees working or involved with the work with ionising radiation and with their representatives;

(g) the ability to keep himself up to date with developments in the use of ionising radiation in the field in which he gives advice, and with developments in radiation protection;

(h) an awareness of legislation, other than that in (d) above, and practices which could affect the work with ionising radiation on which he is expected to give advice;

(i) an appreciation of his own limitations, whether of knowledge, experience, facilities or resources, etc.

Notice of appointment

72 Regulation 10(3)(b) recognises that there may be occasions, e.g. the unforeseen departure or death of the previous RPA, when it will not be possible to give the required 28 days' notice in writing of the intended appointment.

Information and facilities

73 The employer should give the RPA adequate information and facilities to enable him to perform his work effectively. The information should include a clear statement of the scope of the advice the RPA will be required to give. The facilities may need to include the necessary equipment and support services except in the case of an outside consultant who provides his own facilities.

74 In establishments and organisations where there is a potential for serious exposures or substantial contamination and which present special problems and demands for the services of the RPA, then special facilities should be provided to support him. Such facilities should be separate from production and operational units and management.

Matters likely to require RPA consultation

75 When an employer has appointed a radiation protection adviser for the purposes of the Regulations, i.e. the giving of advice, he should consult that RPA about matters that require his expertise, which include:

(a) restriction of exposure and maintenance of engineering controls and other equipment provided for such restriction;

(b) identification of controlled and supervised areas;

(c) control of access to controlled areas;

(d) dosimetry and monitoring;

(e) drawing up written systems of work and local rules;

(f) selection of radiation protection supervisors;

(g) investigation of abnormally high exposures and overexposures;

(h) training;

(i) deciding whether it is feasible to restrict the exposure of female employees to a reasonably uniform rate (see paragraph 67);

(j) hazard assessment and contingency arrangements;

(k) prior examination of any plans for new plant or new premises or modifications to existing plant or premises from a radiation protection aspect;

(l) other aspects of radiation protection that apply to the work with ionising radiation carried on by that employer.

76 Qualified persons appointed for the purposes of Regulation 24 to carry out testing of monitoring instruments need to have the necessary expertise, training and experience to enable them to carry out or supervise the carrying out of the tests to the requirements of that Regulation (see paragraphs 151 to 162).

REGULATION 11
Local rules, supervision and radiation protection supervisors

Local rules

77 Local rules are the general principles and description of the means of complying with the Regulations. They should be set out in writing and as such they should be seen as implementing part of the general safety policy required by Section 2 of the Health and Safety at Work etc. Act 1974.

78 Local rules will vary considerably in detail and format, depending on the complexity of the work with ionising radiations. They may take the form of, or include, instructions, booklets or circulars and written systems of work (see paragraphs 49 to 54) also signs and notices or an explanation of their significance.

79 Generally a complete set of local rules should be held for reference at one central point but copies of the parts of the local rules relevant to the work being undertaken should be made available to the employees directly involved. Alternatively copies may be posted in the sections where the work is undertaken. In both cases all employees who are likely to be directly concerned with the work with ionising radiation should be made aware of the contents of the local rules relevant to the particular operations in which they are involved.

80 The local rules should always contain:

(a) a description of each controlled and supervised area or, where more relevant, the detailed procedure for determining the presence and extent of these areas;

(b) written systems of work detailing the working procedures for non-classified persons who enter controlled areas;

(c) the procedures for restricting access to controlled areas; and

(d) the contingency plans required by Regulation 27.

Radiation protection supervisors

81 The radiation protection supervisor (RPS) plays a supervisory role in assisting the employer to comply with the requirements of the Regulations. He should be directly involved with the work with ionising radiations, preferably in a line management position that will allow him to exercise close supervision to ensure that the work is done in accordance with the local rules, though he need not be present all the time. In some large establishments the RPS may not be the immediate line manager or supervisor overseeing the work with ionising radiation. In these cases a system, which may involve more than one person, should operate to ensure that adequate supervision is maintained.

82   The employer carries the general responsibility of compliance with the Regulations; he cannot delegate that responsibility to the radiation protection supervisor any more than he can to the radiation protection adviser.

83   No person should be appointed as a radiation protection supervisor unless he:
(a) knows and understands the requirements of the Regulations and local rules as they affect the work he supervises;
(b) commands sufficient respect from the people doing the work as will allow him to exercise the necessary supervision of radiation protection; and
(c) understands the necessary precautions to be taken in the work which is being done and the extent to which these precautions will restrict exposures.

REGULATION 12
Information, instruction and training

84   Examples of persons other than employees working with ionising radiation to whom adequate information should be given (see Regulation 12(b)) will include: other workers in the establishment, safety representatives and any persons who might enter a controlled area under a written system of work, e.g. outside contractors. Such people should receive sufficient information to ensure that they do not place themselves or others at risk through ignorance and to enable them to follow relevant local rules.

Information to employees

85   When information is given to employees on risks from exposure to ionising radiation, and in particular to women in respect of the possible risks to the foetus, the employer should include any relevant guidance from the Executive or the appointed doctor.

Training

86   The standard of training to be given to classified persons, trainees and radiation protection supervisors should be appropriate to the nature of the work they are expected to undertake. It is not envisaged that they would all need the standard of training and experience of a radiation protection adviser.

REGULATION 13
Assessment of dose

Assessment of dose

87   A dosimetry service approved under the requirements of Regulation 15 will assess the doses received by employees by making any necessary measurements, examining dosemeters and carrying out the computation of dose. The approved dosimetry service (ADS) will also keep the dose record for the employer. The purpose of the approval system is to ensure as far as possible that the doses are assessed on the basis of accepted national standards.

88   When a person is subject to the requirements for dose assessment, all significant doses (except those received as a result of the person's own medical exposure) are to be assessed. Thus if personal monitors are used they should be worn at all times whilst at work when there is likely to be significant occupational exposure, not just in controlled areas. Where dose assessments are undertaken and it can reasonably be expected that a particular component of dose or committed dose will be less than one-tenth of any appropriate dose limit, then that component would not be regarded as significant and need not be assessed provided that the total of all unassessed components is not likely to exceed one-tenth of any appropriate dose limit.

89   There is a wide variety of methods of assessment of personal dose and the choice of method will depend on the circumstances of individual cases, including the nature of the work and the type of ionising radiations which are to be measured. Examples are: the use of personal dosemeters to assess the whole body dose and skin dose for external radiation; specially designed dosemeters for the dose to the hands; excreta analysis for internal radiation, etc. The methods to adopt should be chosen in consultation with both the radiation protection adviser and the approved dosimetry service.

90 The period between changing dosemeters should be chosen in relation to the dose rates, dose quantity likely to be received in the period and the sensitivity of the personal dosemeter. Intervals of one month are normal but shorter or longer intervals may be necessary. Intervals as long as three months would only be appropriate where small dose quantities are being assessed.

Arrangements with the approved dosimetry service(s)

91 Although the duty is on the employer, in practice it is expected that the dosimetry arrangements will be agreed between the approved dosimetry service, the employer and the radiation protection adviser. All are expected to be involved in putting the arrangements into operation. It is unlikely that the ADS would itself hand out personal dosemeters to the employees: this would more than likely be done by the employer. Similarly the employer would probably have a part to play in taking air samples. Nevertheless the ADS has to be fully in agreement with the arrangements, which may well vary for different employers. The ADS will also need to be kept informed of any changes in circumstances that might affect the arrangements.

92 The employer should arrange to receive summaries of the dose record at least once every 3 months. He should also arrange to be notified by the ADS at any time when the dose quantity received by any employee is approaching any level that, if exposure continued, would require either the employer or the ADS to take some action, e.g. at three-tenths of the dose limit for workers over 18, or three-fifths of that dose limit in any calendar quarter, or any dose limit.

93 If an employee to whom the Regulation applies transfers from one employer to another and remains subject to Regulation 13, the dosimetry should be continued so that the total dose received in the period concerned is assessed. Continuity will not normally mean retaining the same dosemeter at the transfer.

94 In some cases more than one ADS may be needed because of different dosimetry requirements, e.g. one might carry out external radiation dosimetry for exposure to gamma radiation and another might carry out internal radiation dosimetry for exposure to tritium. The employer should make arrangements with one of the ADSs to co-ordinate the dosimetry work carried out by the other ADSs that are involved in dose assessments for that employer.

REGULATION 14
Accident dosimetry

95 In cases to which Regulation 14(1)(c) applies, appropriate means for the assessment of dose may be:

(a) examination of biological specimens, e.g. hair, fingernails, blood, etc;

(b) computation of dose from measured dose rates or contamination levels together with a knowledge of exposure time and distance from places of measurement; and

(c) any other method which could give a reasonably reliable estimate of the dose.

REGULATION 16
Medical surveillance

Health record

96 A form, which specifies the approved particulars to be contained in the health record of employees for the purposes of Regulation 16(2), is available from HMSO. Where an alternative form of health record is used it should contain at least all the particulars specified in the official form. Confidential clinical information is not appropriate to the health record required by this Regulation.

97 When dose rates to the abdomen are not likely to exceed 13 mSv in any 3-month interval (see also paragraph 67) and the employer has completed the relevant part of the health record to that effect before each review, the question of whether that employee is a woman of reproductive capacity does not arise for the purpose of medical surveillance.

Purpose of medical surveillance

98 The primary purpose of medical surveillance is to ensure, before persons are classified, that they are fit to commence such work and that periodically reviews are made to see that they remain fit. Under Regulation 9(3) a person cannot be a classified person unless he has been certified fit by the Employment Medical Adviser (EMA) or Appointed Doctor (AD) in the health record. It should be noted that such a certification of fitness is specific to work with ionising radiations and should not therefore be interpreted as concerning itself with other requirements of the job.

Provision of suitable facilities

99 Facilities which are acceptable to the EMA or AD will need to be provided to enable him to carry out the medical surveillance of the persons concerned. When these are not provided at the place of employment the employer should arrange for the employee to attend a place acceptable to the EMA or AD (e.g. his surgery or examination room). The employer should bear the full cost, including time off for attendance.

Adequate medical surveillance

100 Adequate medical surveillance includes:

(a) pre-employment medical examinations;

(b) special medical examinations;

(c) periodic reviews of health; and

(d) determining whether further dose limit conditions are appropriate.

101 Medical surveillance would not be considered to be adequate unless, following an investigation carried out under Regulation 29 which showed that any person at work had received a dose of ionising radiation in excess of twice any of the annual dose limits for employees aged 18 or over, the person concerned (irrespective of his age) had without delay undergone a special medical examination.

102 Periodic reviews of health should take place at least once in every period of 12 months after the pre-employment medical examination or previous review, or such shorter time as the EMA and AD may specify in the health record. The format of this review will be a matter of judgement on the part of the EMA or AD and may involve, for example, assessment of a dose profile, an interview with the individual, a full medical examination, medical tests and exceptionally chromosome aberration tests.

Change of employment

103 When a classified person has changed employment and is to be classified by the new employer, a pre-employment medical examination need not take place if the person has been certified fit within the preceding 12 months and a copy of that certification has been obtained and kept in the new health record for that person. Any conditions already imposed would continue to have effect until the next periodic review.

104 On change of employment the EMA or AD may, with the co-operation of the previous EMA or AD, also use previously obtained clinical information, e.g. chest X-ray, to avoid unnecessary duplication.

REGULATION 18
Sealed sources and articles containing or embodying radioactive substances

Prevention of dispersal of radioactive substances

105 This Regulation applies in principle to all sealed sources and articles containing radioactive substances. The purpose of the Regulation is to ensure that the risks of dispersal of radioactive substances are minimised.

106 The employer should ensure that the bonding, immediate container or other mechanical protection of the radioactive substance is fully fit for the intended use. Whilst suppliers have a duty to provide information, which would include the strengths and characteristics of the materials and devices used, the employer should consider the circumstances of use, manipulation, storage or transportation within his work, so as to assure himself that the manufacturing specification suits the purposes which he has in mind.

Suitable tests

107 A suitable test for leakage is one which:

(a) has regard for the nature of the source or article;

(b) uses a method which specifies pass/fail criteria; and

(c) conforms to the test methods set out in British Standard BS 5288: 1976, Appendix D, *Specification for Sealed Radioactive Sources*. An alternative test method specified by the manufacturer or supplier of the source or articles, providing that he is subject to the provisions of Regulation 32 and to Section 6 of the Health and Safety at Work etc. Act 1974, could be adopted but only where the test methods specified in British Standard BS 5288: 1976 are inappropriate to that source or article.

108 Tests for leakage should ideally be carried out on the source capsule or container but in deciding whether to do such a direct test the following points should be taken into account:

(a) the accessibility of the source; and

(b) the dose which would be received by the person undertaking a direct test compared with that if an indirect method was used.

If an indirect test is carried out then it should be on parts that could reasonably be expected to reveal any leakage from the source.

Limitations on testing

109 Tests on any source or article which has no dimension greater than 5 mm may not be appropriate. Such a source may be treated as a dispersible radioactive substance: examples are gold grains and microspheres. However, this should not preclude leak tests being carried out on smaller sources where it is feasible. It is not considered appropriate to carry out leak tests to the standards set out in paragraph 107 in the following circumstances:

(a) where the sealed source contains solely gaseous radioactive substances;

(b) where the instantaneous dose rate at or near the surface of any sealed source (i.e. measured as near the surface as practicable for the purposes of measuring ionising radiation) does not exceed $100\,\mu\text{Svh}^{-1}$;

(c) on an article containing a radioactive substance which is solely designed and used for the purpose of detecting smoke or fire and is installed in a building for that purpose;

(d) an article where the radioactive substance, not being a sealed source, is by design open, e.g. a syringe, bottle or similar equipment; and

(e) any sealed sources during irradiation in a nuclear reactor (see definition of sealed source in Regulation 2).

Care should be taken with all radioactive substances to prevent contamination whether or not leakage tests are carried out. In the case of anti-static devices containing microspheres where leak tests may not be appropriate, a periodic check should be made to ensure that contamination has not occurred.

Suitable interval for leak tests

110 A suitable interval for leak tests will in most cases be 26 months. Additional tests should be made when damage is suspected or when maintenance is carried out which could affect the integrity of the source. The frequency of testing should be increased where the physical or chemical conditions to which the source is subjected are such that deterioration of the source or its containment might occur.

Suitable record

111 The following information constitutes a suitable record:

(a) name and address of the person or organisation responsible for carrying out the leak test;

(b) means of identifying the source or article;

(c) date of test;

17

(d) reason for test (i.e. pre-use, manufacturer's test, normal routine, after incident);

(e) methods of test (including statement of pass/fail criteria);

(f) numerical results of the test;

(g) result of test (pass or fail);

(h) remedial action taken if failure occurred;

(i) name and signature of person carrying out the test.

**REGULATION 19
Accounting for
radioactive
substances**

112 Accounting procedures should be such as to ensure that the whereabouts of radioactive substances are known and losses of significant quantities are identified quickly.

113 The records for accounting for any particular radioactive substance should contain:

(a) a means of identification which should, in the case of a sealed source, be unique;

(b) the date of receipt;

(c) the activity at a specified date;

(d) the whereabouts of the source updated at appropriate intervals (see paragraph 114); and

(e) the date and manner of disposal (when appropriate).

114 In paragraph 113(d), the intervals at which the updates should be carried out will be dependent on the likely movement of the source, its potential for being displaced and its susceptibility to damage. Examples of intervals are:

(a) for portable radiography sources, portable gauges, etc, the check should be at least on each working day;

(b) for static sources securely attached to machines the frequency may be up to 1 month, providing that additional checks are carried out following any maintenance or repair which could have affected the source; and

(c) for sources located within patients, the interval should also be compatible with the clinical treatment of that patient.

115 Very small sources or articles having no dimension greater than 5 mm may be treated for the purposes of accounting as dispersible radioactive substances.

116 Accounting procedures need not be adopted for any radioactive substance having a half life of less than 3 hours or in the form of contamination, nor where the quantity of a discrete source or confined radioactive substance is less than the quantity specified in column 2 of Schedule 2; this does not relieve the employer of the duties imposed by any other of these Regulations.

117 Accounting procedures may be suspended for a radioactive substance whilst it is undergoing irradiation in a nuclear reactor, particle accelerator or other similar device, provided that any such radioactive substance is not directly related to the operation of the plant.

118 The need to account for radioactive substances which form part of a nuclear reactor arises when radioactive components are removed or when the reactor is de-commissioned.

119 For all other radioactive substances, accounting procedures should where appropriate give the detail set out in paragraph 113. In determining what is appropriate the following may be taken into account:

(a) the accounting procedure may disregard such materials as are dispersed in the body of a person, except that samples taken from such persons which contain a quantity in excess of the quantity in column 2 of Schedule 2 would constitute a discrete radioactive substance and should thus be accounted for if kept for more than 24 hours;

(b) in production processes directly involving dispersible radioactive substances the accounting procedures will vary considerably with the scale of operation. In most cases the records held for production processing and waste disposal would be sufficient; and

18

(c) in small scale laboratories it would be sufficient to know the activity present and the radionuclides involved in each room, supported by the records required for waste disposal purposes.

120 Where in the nuclear industry there are large quantities of radioactive substances and the means of accounting involves estimates which may be subject to uncertainties because of the quantities involved, an apparent loss could be indicated requiring notification under Regulation 31. In such cases an agreement may be reached with the Executive at local level as to what accountancy error is sufficiently large to constitute reasonable grounds for believing that the radioactive substance has been lost.

121 An annual check should be carried out to ensure that the accounting record is a true record. Such a check necessarily excludes any radioactive substances which have decayed to an insignificant quantity.

REGULATION 20
Keeping of
radioactive
substances

122 Radioactive substances should be kept in a suitable receptacle when not in use, amongst other reasons to ensure effective restriction of exposure to ionising radiations, control against dispersal and security. Different criteria apply when a radioactive substance is being transported or moved (see paragraphs 128 and 129). The following matters are some of those which should be taken into account in deciding whether a receptacle is suitable:

(a) the corrosiveness of the radioactive substance;

(b) the self-heating effect in high activity sources;

(c) the pyrophoricity of the radioactive substance;

(d) any anticipated pressure build-up inside the receptacle;

(e) the degree of fire resistance of the receptacle (see paragraph 124);

(f) the dispersibility of the radioactive substance, e.g. powders should be sealed in a container such as a plastic bag and placed in another container to prevent damage to the bag and provide shielding;

(g) the corrosiveness of the storage environment;

(h) the need to provide shielding from ionising radiation emitted by the radioactive substance so that the dose rate does not exceed $2 \, \text{mSvh}^{-1}$ at the receptacle surface. In many cases lower dose rates will need to be achieved under the requirements of Regulation 6;

(i) whether the construction of the receptacle is such that it will withstand damage from foreseeable use or misuse; and

(j) whether the security of the receptacle is such that it will prevent unauthorised exposure or dispersal.

123 When a radioactive substance cannot be placed in a suitable receptacle other equivalent protection should be provided; for example, a girder containing induced activity may, because of its size, have to be stored in the open where it should be covered (e.g. wrapped in polythene sheeting) to protect it from the weather so as to prevent the production of radioactive rust which could cause contamination.

124 A suitable store for radioactive substances should provide:

(a) protection from the effects of the weather;

(b) resistance to fire sufficient to minimise dispersal and minimise loss of shielding, taking into account the combustibility of surrounding materials and the likely temperatures that would be reached in the event of a fire;

(c) shielding to achieve outside the store the lowest instantaneous dose rate that is reasonably practicable. Where non-classified persons may approach the outside of the store the instantaneous dose rate should not normally exceed $2.5 \, \mu\text{Svh}^{-1}$. Where this figure is exceeded consideration should be given to whether the area needs to be designated as a controlled or supervised area;

(d) ventilation to prevent significant accumulations of gases and vapours (whether radioactive or not) or of any accidentally dispersed radioactive substance; and

(e) proper physical security such that access is only normally possible to those persons permitted by the employer, whether or not the inside of the store is a controlled area.

125 Any store allocated to radioactive substances should be reserved for such substances, their immediate containers and receptacles and immediately ancillary items such as handling tools and shielding material. In particular, nothing explosive or highly flammable should be kept in the store.

126 A sign should be prominently displayed outside the store (preferably on the door) to warn persons in the vicinity that the store may contain radioactive substances. The signs should conform to the Safety Signs Regulations 1980 and to British Standards BS 3510: 1968 and BS 5378: 1980.

REGULATION 21
Transport and moving of radioactive substances

Definition

127 Transport commences the moment that a radioactive substance is loaded onto a conveyance and ceases only when it is taken off. Where a radioactive substance is transported by hand Regulation 21 only applies whilst the substance is in a public place. If a substance is not by definition being transported then the requirements relating to the movement of radioactive substances should be applied.

Suitable receptacle

128 A suitable receptacle for the transport of radioactive substances is one that satisfies the packaging and labelling requirements contained in the current requirements of the International Atomic Energy Agency (IAEA) in relation to the safe transport of radioactive materials.

129 A receptacle which satisfies paragraph 128 can be taken to be suitable for the purpose of moving a radioactive substance. If a receptacle does not meet those requirements then the following matters should be taken into account in deciding whether it is suitable for this purpose:

(a) the adequacy of the shielding for the person moving the radioactive substance;

(b) the distance through which the receptacle will be moved;

(c) the likely hazards to be encountered and the consequences of an incident, e.g. whether the receptacle gives adequate protection against spill or dispersal; and

(d) the physical and chemical form and the activity of the radioactive substance.

130 A suitable receptacle for the transport or movement of a live animal containing a radioactive substance is one that provides adequate shielding and containment having made allowance for the well-being of the animal.

Controlled areas

131 Consideration of controlled areas around sources of ionising radiation whilst they are being moved or transported is dealt with in paragraphs 41 and 45.

Information

132 The information which should accompany a radioactive substance being transported should include:

(a) a description of the radioactive substance, e.g. the radioisotope, its quantity and physical form;

(b) a statement to the effect that it is packaged and labelled in accordance with IAEA requirements or is exempt; and

(c) any additional information which would be required to enable the person opening it to do so safely.

REGULATION 22
Washing and changing facilities

133 The type of work that is carried out with radioactive substances and the nature and likely levels of contamination, bearing in mind accidental spillages or other similar mishaps, will influence the decision on what facilities should be provided for washing and/or changing.

134 The provision of washing facilities will be necessary for places where contamination is likely; what is adequate will vary from normal washing facilities where only low levels are expected, to showers. The facilities should be sited so that contamination is not spread beyond the area for which they are provided and should be adjacent to changing facilities where these are provided.

135 Washing facilities should at least include wash basins with hot and cold water supplied via jets or sprays which, for controlled areas, can be operated without using hands (e.g. foot or elbow operated). There should also be soap, nail brushes and drying facilities such as disposable towels. Static or roller towels are not suitable.

136 Arrangements should be made for leaving any protective clothing or respiratory protective equipment that has been worn or used, or any other clothing that may have been contaminated, in the controlled or supervised area. The arrangements should prevent the spread of contamination to 'clean' clothes. In controlled and supervised areas where clothing is changed or respiratory protective equipment is used the following should be provided:

(a) a bench, barrier or other means of demarcation at the exit from the area, designed so that any protective clothing and respiratory protective equipment which may be contaminated can be removed and left within the area (see also paragraphs 22 to 25);

(b) lockers or other arrangements, such that each person can leave clothing, shoes, etc, worn in uncontaminated areas on the 'clean' side of the bench or barrier and leave on the 'active' side any protective clothing and equipment used in areas where there may be contamination. In laboratories handling small quantities of radioactive substances less onerous arrangements are acceptable, provided that cross contamination of clean clothes/shoes is effectively prevented;

(c) containers on the 'active' side of the barrier for discarded contaminated clothing; and

(d) monitoring facilities so that employees and other persons can check body surfaces and clothing for contamination (see also paragraphs 32 and 145).

REGULATION 23
Personal protective equipment

137 The purpose of a thorough examination is to establish that the item being examined is fit for the use to which it is to be put, that physical deterioration has not occurred and that it has not become contaminated since its last thorough examination.

138 The interval between thorough examinations will be dependant on the type of equipment, the hazard against which it is required to protect, the conditions under which it is used, the likelihood of deterioration, the extent to which it could become contaminated and the frequency of use.

139 If the radiation protection consequences of failure of the equipment are likely to be serious the frequency of thorough examination should be increased, e.g. pressurised suits and overshoes used in heavily contaminated areas should be examined between each time of use. In appropriate circumstances an alternative would be to use disposable equipment.

140 For most operations the interval between thorough inspections for respiratory protective equipment should not exceed 1 month. For self-contained positive pressure respiratory protective equipment the examinations should be thorough and should include a check on the condition of the air supply. For respiratory protective equipment that is kept in sealed packs it should be sufficient to see that no obvious deterioration has taken place or, alternatively, the examination should take place between each time it is used, provided that a quality control check is carried out at least annually.

141 For equipment having less radiation protection consequences the examination could be less frequent, with intervals perhaps even extending up to 12 months for items such as lead gloves or lead aprons.

142 Records of examination are only required in respect of respiratory protective equipment and should contain the means of identification and condition of the equipment, the date of examination and the signature of the person who carried it out. As an alternative, where large numbers of similar items of respiratory protective equipment are involved, the employer may wish to adopt a dating system that ensures that the date of the last examination is known or can be worked out.

REGULATION 24
Monitoring of levels for radiation and contamination

143 Monitoring is one important means of indicating whether levels of radiation and of contamination are satisfactory for continuing the work with ionising radiation, detecting breakdowns in controls or systems and detecting changes in levels of radiation. Thus monitoring needs to take place outside controlled and supervised areas as well as inside in order to check that such places remain correctly designated.

144 Monitoring should also be used to determine radiation levels and contamination arising from particular operations or situations so that control measures can be determined for the purpose of complying with Regulation 6.

145 The provision of personnel contamination monitors (e.g. hand and foot monitors) for controlled or supervised areas may provide part of the overall monitoring system; when such monitors are provided they should conform to the testing and maintenance requirements of this Regulation (see also paragraphs 32 and 136(d)).

146 In order to establish whether adequate monitoring is being achieved the following should be considered:

(a) what kinds of measurements should be made (e.g. dose rates, surface contamination, air concentrations);

(b) where the measurements should be made;

(c) how frequently or on what occasions these measurements should be made (including measurements forming part of contingency arrangements, see Regulation 27);

(d) what method of measurement, e.g. direct measurement with an instrument, collection of air samples, use of wipe samples (see paragraph 147 concerning wipe samples);

(e) who should carry out the measurements;

(f) what records should be kept (see paragraph 159);

(g) reference levels and the action to be taken if they are exceeded; and

(h) when the monitoring procedures should be reviewed.

Wipe tests

147 When monitoring for surface contamination distinction may need to be made between fixed and loose contamination (see paragraph 58). One method which may be used to assess the extent of loose contamination is to wipe the surface with an absorbent material and assume that one-tenth of the removable contamination has been transferred to the absorbent material from the area over which the material has been wiped, unless that fraction is capable of being determined. Care needs to be exercised when using this assumption, particularly if the chemical form of the contamination is one that can be absorbed directly through the skin.

Provision of suitable monitoring equipment

148 Where conditions are not expected to change and when only low output sources are present employers may share monitoring equipment, provided that this does not interfere with any monitoring procedures that need to be undertaken.

149 The suitability of monitoring equipment relates to the matching of the equipment to the type, nature, intensity and energy of the radiation that has to be monitored and to the conditions of use. This matching process should be achieved by tests carried out before the equipment is taken into use.

Role of the radiation protection adviser(s) and qualified person(s)

150 When drawing up a monitoring regime the employer should consult his radiation protection adviser.

151 Any qualified person appointed for the purpose of Regulation 24(3) to carry out or supervise tests should possess the required expertise in instrumentation, theory and practice. He should be fully conversant with, and have knowledge and understanding of, currently accepted testing standards and relevant British Calibration Service technical guidance in relation to testing the monitoring equipment that he is expected to test. This knowledge and understanding should include being able to estimate the accuracy of calibration against known standards (see paragraph 158).

Testing instruments before use

152 Testing of instruments before they are taken into use should comprise individual tests of each monitoring instrument and individual calibration. These tests are to establish the instrument's performance for its intended use and also to determine any limitations that may render it unsuitable for certain applications. Information on the limitations of any equipment and its accuracy of calibration should be available to any person who uses or may use it.

153 Where, as part of the service to employers, manufacturers, suppliers or firms and organisations specialising in monitoring equipment carry out the tests referred to in Regulation 24(2), then this arrangement will be acceptable if the tests are carried out by, or under the immediate supervision of, a qualified person appointed for this purpose (qualified persons can be appointed by such bodies). The qualified person will be able to decide on the testing required in the light of any reliable information he has about the design criteria and performance characteristics of that particular type of equipment, and of its intended use. Such information may be available as a result of type testing carried out to accepted standards by or under the control of a qualified person or carried out in a British Calibration Service accredited laboratory.

154 Where type testing has been carried out the only individual testing that needs to be done is a selected set of tests to verify that the instrument conforms to the type, followed by the individual calibration. Where no type test has been carried out, at least one of any batch of identical instruments should be fully tested. A similar set of individual tests should suffice for the remainder. All instruments should be individually calibrated before use.

155 In the case of imported equipment, the qualified person undertaking the individual tests before use will need to be satisfied that any foreign type test matches up to currently accepted standards before he can accept that only a selected set of tests for verification to type will suffice to enable the employer to fulfil the requirements of Regulation 24(2).

Periodic examination and testing

156 The purpose of the regular thorough examination and test is to ensure that the equipment is not damaged, has not lost its calibration and is suitable for the expected duration of use before its next thorough examination and test. Any faults or potential faults that are identified should be rectified: it may be necessary to retest the calibration following any repair. Similarly if the calibration has changed significantly then a full re-calibration should be carried out.

157 Most thorough examinations and tests are likely to be undertaken by organisations and individuals specialising in this work but there is no reason why an employer should not do his own, provided that he has a qualified person with the necessary expertise and facilities to carry out the tests.

Accuracy of calibration

158 All calibrations should make use of sources or equipment that ensure a known accuracy of calibration in relation to appropriate national standards. In many cases this will involve the use of sources whose activity has been determined to a known

23

accuracy, e.g. one obtained from a British Calibration Service accredited laboratory, or the use of equipment that has been previously calibrated to known accuracy. One method of achieving this would be to follow any relevant British Calibration Service technical guidance for conducting tests on monitoring instruments.

Suitable records

159   Records which should be kept are those which confirm that controlled and supervised areas are correctly designated and located and those which show that levels are being approached which may require investigatory or remedial action to be taken. There may be no need to retain many routine results of monitoring.

160   The record of the results of monitoring should include the date, time, place, radiation level found, i.e. dose rate, air concentration or surface contamination and the conditions existing where relevant in relation to the radiation level measured.

161   A suitable record of the tests of monitoring equipment should include: identification of the equipment, the calibration accuracy over its range of operation for the types of radiation that it is intended to monitor, the date of the test and the name and signature of the qualified person under whose direction the test was carried out.

Checks in use

162   Battery checks, zeroing and tests for lack of response should be carried out at frequent intervals to ensure that the equipment is still functioning satisfactorily and has suffered no obvious damage.

REGULATION 25
Assessment of hazards

163   This Regulation applies, without exception, to all employers who carry out work with ionising radiations. The reason for making the assessment is essentially threefold: it should enable the employer to take what steps are required to prevent the foreseeable accidents occurring, to limit their consequences and to prepare the contingency plan required under Regulation 27.

164   There is no legal requirement that the assessment has to be written until inventories of radioactive substances reach those of large scale users and transport operators, when Regulation 26 specifies what is required. However it is clear that some matters will need to be written down and kept with the local rules. Assessments should be carried out by all employers who work with ionising radiations; these may range from small users with relatively insignificant hazards such as a single gauge or a single X-ray set, to persons working with multiple sources. In the case of large medical therapy sources a written assessment would always be desirable because of the large dose rates that would be present in the event of loss of shielding, even though the risk of dispersal could be minimal or non-existent.

165   A generic assessment, which described the radiation hazard in terms that would apply in any place or at any time, would be reasonable in circumstances where accidents, albeit on different occasions, would give rise to similar radiation conditions: a transport operation moving similar loads, or an industrial radiography business involved in taking their own sources or radiation generators from site to site are examples where this applies. In these cases a separate assessment would not be expected for each occasion or site.

166   The matters which will need to be considered when an employer carries out a hazard assessment will include the likely breakdown of systems of work, the probability of failure of plant and control systems, the likelihood of transport accidents and the likely consequences of any accident or incident.

167   When considering what is a reasonably foreseeable accident the bizarre need not be taken into account. However if, for example, the substances were on a site which was situated on a regular flight landing path the effects of a crash should be considered, as should the effects of a road crash or loss of a source from a holder or remote operation cable in the case of peripatetic industrial radiographers.

REGULATION 27
Contingency plans

168   The choice of a suitable dosemeter or other device (for issue under Regulation 27(4)(b)) will need to take account of the types of radiation and the likely dose quantities which could be received. In some situations a routine dosemeter may be suitable, in others a different type, such as a criticality dosemeter, may be more appropriate.

169   Where fissile materials are present the contingency plan should take the possibility of criticality excursions into account. Criticality alarms should form a properly designed system that allows for failure of components and the system should be properly maintained.

170   For the purpose of Regulation 27(3)(c), the persons who should be named are those who actually carry out tasks associated with the plan.

REGULATION 28
Investigation of exposure

171   The intention of this provision is to trigger a procedure for ensuring that all due steps are being taken to keep the exposure of groups or individuals, engaged in essentially similar tasks in essentially the same environment, to the lowest reasonably practicable level. Thus one investigation would be necessary for one group of similar workers. If an investigation has been carried out in a previous year and that investigation showed that the employer was restricting exposure so far as was reasonably practicable, it would be sufficient for him to review that investigation and identify whether any changes in the previous conclusions should be made.

172   Particular scrutiny should be applied to any groups or individuals who consistently exceed the 15 mSv level and to any individual who approaches dose limits. In situations where an employer takes on a new employee who has already received a dose in that calendar year, the current employer should assume the responsibility for carrying out the investigation under this Regulation only in so far as it involves his own work.

REGULATION 29
Investigation and notification of overexposure

173   The Regulation applies to any overexposure, as defined, or suspected overexposure whether it arises from a single incident or because the total of doses received by the person during the period in question exceeds any dose limit for that period. No account should be taken of any doses received as medical exposures.

REGULATION 30
Dose limitation for overexposed employees

174   An employer may allow an employee who has received an overexposure to continue to work with ionising radiation, providing that:

(a) the provisions of Regulation 29(1) have been complied with; and

(b) the work is performed in accordance with any conditions imposed by an employment medical adviser or appointed doctor under Regulation 16(6).

REGULATION 31
Notification of certain occurrences

175   A radioactive substance is under the control of the employer who is in charge of it, in control of what is done with it, or in control of how it is used at that time. In the context of this Regulation, release should be taken to include accidental spillages of radioactive substances, such as bench spills in a laboratory.

176   To assist in determining whether an occurrence involving the release of a solid radioactive substance is likely to give rise to a quantity of dust which exceeds the quantity specified in column 7 of Schedule 2 of the Regulations it is reasonable to assume that one-thousandth of the total amount of material involved in the occurrence will be released into the atmosphere. This assumption cannot be applied where:

(a) an exceptionally fine dust is involved;

(b) other information is available to show that the assumption is not appropriate, i.e. where the release is under pressure or caused by an explosion; or

(c) a solid piece or block of radioactive substance is involved.

177   For the purpose of Regulation 31(1)(b) contamination should be regarded as significant if either of the following conditions applies:

(a) the surface contamination exceeds 100 times the quantity in column 4 of Schedule 2 of the Regulations when averaged over 1000 cm^2; or

(b) the instantaneous dose rate measured at 1 m above the contaminated surface is greater than 1 mSvh^{-1};

but not where the spillage is in an enclosure or other facility which is designed and maintained to effectively prevent a release beyond that facility.

REGULATION 32
Duties of manufacturers, etc, of articles or substances for use in work with ionising radiation

178   All persons involved in the chain from the design, to the supply, to the use or installation of an article have a responsibility to ensure that clear, unambiguous and comprehensive information is passed along that chain. Only then can the user know precisely how the article should be used so that the standards of restriction of exposure and compliance with the Regulations can be maintained or improved, commensurate with the article performing the function for which it was intended.

179   Sometimes a commercially available article that was neither designed for use in connection with work with ionising radiations, nor sold by the supplier for that purpose, is nevertheless used as such by an employer working with ionising radiations: one example would be an extractor fan bought merely as a fan of known capacity from a retailer and then incorporated into a ventilation system intended to control airborne radioactive substances. Unless an article has been supplied on the basis of its future use or its design criteria the employer should ensure that it complies with the Regulations and achieves the necessary performance standard.

180   The manufacturer, supplier or importer of any article embodying or containing a radioactive substance, including a sealed source, should ensure that suitable leak tests are carried out as soon as practicable after manufacture or importation.

181   It is appropriate to carry out a critical examination of the way in which an article is being or has been erected or installed if there are radiation protection implications. This may be carried out in the course of supply, erection/installation, commissioning, or trials prior to normal use and may require co-operation (see Regulation 4) between the various employers involved at each stage.

182   A critical examination should be carried out for articles containing radioactive substances and for radiation generators. Other articles which may form part of plant should also be covered by the critical examination. This should take into account matters such as shielding, ease of decontamination of surfaces, containment and any other aspects of radiation protection.

REGULATION 33
Equipment used for medical exposure

183   The detailed guidance given in Part 2 of this Code relating to medical exposures and the persons who work with patients should be read in conjunction with this section.

Regulation 33(1)

184   This paragraph covers all equipment used in connection with medical exposures where the design, construction, installation, maintenance, and any fault that might develop in it, can affect the magnitude of the absorbed dose received by the patient. Ancillary equipment should therefore be designed, constructed, installed and maintained with a view to restricting exposure. In this context ancillary equipment such as image receptors, intensifying screens, beam filters, isotope calibrators and film processing units is included, as the design and maintenance affects the dose given to the patient.

185   X-ray beams should be adjusted so that the useful beam is directed away from adjacent areas that are occupied but inadequately shielded and should be restricted and collimated to the minimum size necessary. Filtration should be provided to remove unwanted components from the radiation beam directed towards persons undergoing medical exposure, consistent with the intended clinical result. This paragraph may also be relevant to the protection of persons who carry out radiography.

REGULATION 35
Defence on contravention of certain Regulations

186 Regulations 5(4), 17(1) and 26(4) enable the Executive to require employers to do certain things. Regulation 35 has effect to introduce an appeal procedure by providing a defence where an inspector may use section 21 of the Health and Safety at Work etc. Act 1974 to issue an improvement notice before commencing any proceedings under the Regulations.

PART 2 Applications of Regulation 6 to specified processes

Introduction

The material in this part of the Code is additional to that given in Part 1 which still applies to the processes dealt with in the following sections.

SECTION 1
Diagnostic radiology using X-ray equipment for medical exposures and in veterinary practice

Scope

1 This section of the Code applies to:

(a) any use of X-ray equipment where the primary use of that X-ray equipment is for examination of patients and human corpses by radiography, fluoroscopy, xeroradiography, computed tomography, and similar processes, or for such examinations of animals in veterinary practice, medical research, or veterinary research;

(b) any use of X-ray equipment where that X-ray equipment is primarily used for training persons in the techniques of diagnostic examination of persons or animals or for research into those techniques; and

(c) the testing of, or the measurement of radiation produced by, any X-ray equipment mentioned at (a) or (b) above, where that testing or measurement is carried out in the premises where the X-ray equipment is normally used.

Segregation of the work activity

2 The work should be carried out in a room or enclosure that provides adequate shielding (see paragraph 13 of Part 1 of this Code). All persons who are not directly concerned with the work should be excluded.

3 If the work cannot be carried out in a special facility because of practical or clinical considerations, e.g. in domiciliary or ward radiography, then the area in which it is done should have all unnecessary persons excluded during the exposure. In deciding whether patients in adjacent beds should be moved in ward radiography the following points should be taken into account:

(a) the clinical implications of moving them; and

(b) the increase in dose over what they may have already received as a medical exposure.

Signals

4 A device should be provided which will automatically give a signal to any person operating the main control panel of any X-ray equipment that an X-ray tube is in a state of readiness to emit X-rays.

5 For permanently installed equipment a device should be provided at the entrance to the room which will automatically give a warning signal when any X-ray tube is in a state of readiness to produce X-rays. This warning device should continue to operate all the time that the X-ray tube remains in this state and also when it is emitting radiation.

6 Where it is possible from a single location to initiate the production of X-rays from more than one X-ray tube, each X-ray tube should be provided with means for automatically giving a warning signal whilst that X-ray tube is selected to emit X-rays.

Beam filtration

7 Although filtration is provided primarily to reduce the effects of soft X-rays in persons undergoing a medical exposure, it is also relevant to the protection of other persons (see paragraph 185 of Part 1 of this Code).

Control of X-ray production

8 The means of initiating and terminating the production of X-rays should be such that:
(a) their design reduces the likelihood of X-rays being produced inadvertently;
(b) effective means are provided and maintained for automatically terminating the production of X-rays when the desired exposure is complete;
(c) manual means are provided for isolating the equipment from the electricity supply;
(d) where switches are provided for fluoroscopy they should be so connected that they cannot energise X-ray tubes that are not intended for fluoroscopy;
(e) means are provided and maintained on any fluoroscopic X-ray equipment to ensure that a fluoroscopic exposure is not possible unless the image receptor is correctly positioned with respect to the X-ray tube.

9 The controls which govern the production of X-rays should be clearly and unambiguously indicated.

Avoidance of exposure to the useful beam

10 No person other than a person undergoing examination should be exposed to the useful beam of the X-ray equipment except as indicated in paragraph 11.

11 Only in exceptional circumstances should a patient or animal undergoing a diagnostic examination be supported or manipulated by hand. When a patient is being supported by another person the radiographer should arrange the exposure to avoid that person being in the incident beam. The person supporting or manipulating the patient or animal should wear a protective apron and be as far outside the beam as is practicable. Protective gloves should be worn if the hands are likely at any time to be close to the incident beam. Dosimetric measurements should be made when these procedures are carried out by employees. For persons other than employees, the circumstances in which personal dosemeters should be worn should be described in local rules and any relevant written systems of work as appropriate.

12 Any new fluoroscopy facility, or one which is substantially rebuilt or modified after these Regulations come into force, should be provided with a means of viewing which does not permit direct vision of the fluoroscopy screen. On existing equipment where such facilities are not an integral part of the design, persons should not look directly at any fluoroscopy screen.

SECTION 2
Radiation beam therapy

Scope

13 This section of the Code applies to:
(a) any use of a radiation generator which is primarily for radiation beam therapy of persons or animals;
(b) any use of equipment incorporating one or more radioactive sources, including remotely controlled gamma ray after-loading equipment primarily used for radiation therapy of persons or animals where the instantaneous dose rate in the useful beam exceeds $10\,\mathrm{mSvh}^{-1}$ at 1 m from the source or sources, but excluding any nuclear reactor; and
(c) any use of a radiation generator other than X-ray equipment which is already covered by Section 1 of this Part of the Code and which is used for diagnostic examinations of persons or animals (e.g. neutron generators).

14 This section also applies to:

(a) the testing and measurement of radiation from equipment referred to in paragraph 13; and

(b) the loading and unloading of radioactive sources into the equipment mentioned in paragraph 13(b);

providing that this work is carried out in the premises where the equipment is normally used for the purposes specified in paragraph 13.

Segregation of the work activity

15 The work should be carried out in a room or enclosure which is set apart for the purpose and which provides adequate shielding (see paragraph 13 of Part 1 of this Code. For radiation beam therapy the time average dose rate should not exceed $7.5\,\mu Svh^{-1}$ outside the room or enclosure.

16 All persons except the person undergoing the medical exposure should be excluded from the room or enclosure whilst the useful beam is exposed. Where a person has to enter because of some clinical requirement other than an emergency that person should be a classified person or should enter under a written system of work under Regulation 8(6). Personal dose assessment should always be made. Provisions relating to entry in emergencies should be dealt with under contingency arrangements.

17 The control panel for the equipment should be located outside the room or enclosure. A door or barrier with safety devices fitted should be provided and maintained such that it is not possible to expose the useful beam while the door or barrier is open. Effective arrangements should also be made to ensure that if any door or barrier to the room or enclosure is opened while the useful beam is exposed, the equipment is restored to a safe state and it is only possible to re-initiate the useful beam at the control panel following re-closure of the door or barrier.

18 A barrier provided in accordance with paragraph 17 may, for example, take the form of a photo-electric safety system, the interruption of which operates the devices and arrangements described in that paragraph.

19 If the only source of ionising radiation used is an X-ray machine capable of operating at no more than 50 kV, the stipulations contained in paragraphs 16 and 17 need not be followed provided that all persons whose presence is not necessary are excluded from the room or enclosure while X-rays are being produced and suitable protection is worn by persons who remain inside.

20 Special provisions will need to be made for the loading and unloading of radioactive sources into radiotherapy equipment. Persons who are required to do this work, other than remotely from the outside of the enclosure, should be classified persons who are trained and experienced in such work and operating to a predetermined and authorised system of work, because of the potentially high risks involved.

21 For the protection of persons who may, despite precautions, be shut inside the room or enclosure, an alarm should be provided and one or more of the following:

(a) the means of exit should be so positioned, constructed and maintained that those persons can leave the room or enclosure without delay;

(b) means should be provided and maintained whereby those persons can quickly control all the sources of ionising radiation within the room or enclosure; or

(c) shielding to reduce the instantaneous dose rate to less than $2\,mSvh^{-1}$ should be provided for those persons within the room or enclosure.

22 An automatic warning signal which is clear and unambiguous should be given whilst the equipment is in a state of readiness to emit ionising radiation and either whilst any shutter on such equipment is open or the useful beam of any radioactive source is exposed.

The signal should be perceptible:

(a) inside the room or enclosure;

(b) at any entrance to the room or enclosure; and

(c) to any person operating the control panel.

Termination of the exposure

23 Effective means, including an alternative in case of failure of the normal means, should be provided and maintained for terminating the exposure automatically when the pre-set time has elapsed or when a pre-set quantity of ionising radiation has been delivered.

Avoidance of exposure to the useful beam

24 No person other than the person undergoing the medical exposure should be exposed to the useful beam.

SECTION 3
Diagnostic use of radioactive sources

Scope

25 This section of the Code applies to:

(a) any use of equipment containing a radioactive substance, where the primary use of that equipment is for the diagnostic examination of human subjects including human corpses (e.g. for *in vivo* bone mineralisation studies) or for the examination of live animals in veterinary practice, medical research, or veterinary research; and

(b) the testing of equipment mentioned in (a) above.

It does not apply to radioactive neutron sources.

Provision of shielding

26 Shielding should be provided to attenuate the residual radiation from the useful beam and against scattered radiation to ensure that the instantaneous dose rate at the outside of the shielding does not exceed $7.5\,\mu\mathrm{Svh}^{-1}$.

27 When equipment covered by this section of the Code is not in use, or is not under test, suitable devices such as shutters, covers or plates should be provided and arranged to operate automatically to ensure that no controlled area exists in the immediate vicinity. Where it is not reasonably practicable to arrange automatic operation then a manual system may be used.

Warning signs

28 Equipment should be clearly marked to indicate:

(a) that it contains a radioactive substance; and

(b) whether any shutter, cover or plate is open or shut.

Avoidance of exposure to the useful beam

29 No person other than a person undergoing a medical exposure should be exposed to the useful beam of the equipment.

SECTION 4
Radioactive substances used in or on the body

Scope

30 This section applies where a patient has been subject to a medical exposure and as a result has become a source of ionising radiations. It continues to apply in the event of the death of such patients. The guidance in this section is concerned with the radiation protection of any person who comes near to such a patient; it does not apply to the particular patient who is being treated.

Restriction of exposure to ionising radiation

31 The persons other than employees in the establishment (hospital, clinic, etc) who should be restricted from exposure can be thought of as being in two categories:

(a) other patients; and

(b) all other persons.

The degree of restriction of dose to other patients may be influenced by the consideration of what significance the dose would have in relation to that individual's personal circumstances. For example, a proportionately small further accumulation of dose to a radiotherapy patient from an adjacent radioactive patient may not be significant but would almost certainly be so to a young patient who was not to undergo medical exposure.

32   In restricting exposure to employees and visitors the effects of grouping several radioactive patients together in the same place should be taken fully into account when applying the Regulations and the guidance in Part 1 of this Code. In particular, if waiting-rooms require designation as controlled areas visitors should only enter in accordance with the conditions of the written system of work.

33   When a person leaves an establishment with radioactive substances remaining in or on his body, the employer usually loses direct control over the exposure of other persons who have contact with that person. The employer should take the following action in respect of such persons who leave the establishment following medical exposure involving administered or implanted radioactive substances:

(a) identify any critical groups of employees or members of the public who, it is foreseen, may come near to such persons and whose resulting exposure may be significant;

(b) determine any steps that may be required to restrict the exposure of those critical groups; and

(c) incorporate in local rules (see Regulation 11) arrangements to enable the steps referred to above to be taken.

SECTION 5
X-ray baggage and postal inspection systems

Scope

34   This section applies to baggage and postal inspection systems using radiation generators.

Provision of shielding

35   Shielding should be provided to attenuate the residual radiation from the useful beam and against scattered radiation such that the instantaneous dose rate at or near any external surface of the equipment or at any accessible opening is as low as reasonably practicable. Where such equipment is used in a place to which members of the public have access the instantaneous dose rate should not exceed $1\,\mu\text{Svh}^{-1}$.

Signals

36   An automatic visible warning signal should be provided at the operating panel to indicate when the equipment is switched on such that X-rays could be produced and it should continue to operate whilst the equipment is switched on. An additional warning signal that can clearly be seen from any of the openings should be provided. The meaning of the warning signals should be made clear and unambiguous, e.g. by the use of notices.

Control of X-ray production

37   On automatic feed equipment where the presence of the article to be inspected triggers the X-ray production or where the X-rays are produced constantly during use, then isolation of the conveyor should prevent the production of the X-rays. Such means of isolation should be provided at a point convenient for the feed and discharge openings and in some cases also on the panel.

Avoidance of exposure to the useful beam

38   Access should be prevented at the feed and discharge openings such that a person should not be able to reach into any area when the instantaneous dose rate exceeds $7.5\,\mu\text{Svh}^{-1}$. The means of achieving this could be either by the design and layout or by the provision of safety devices such as photoelectric systems and interlocking electrical switches fitted to the doors.

39 All fluoroscopic devices should be provided with viewing facilities which do not permit direct vision of the fluoroscopy screen.

SECTION 6
Non-medical radiography and irradiation (including research)

Scope

40 This section of the Code applies to the following processes:

(a) any use of a radiation generator or sealed source equipment in radiography, fluoroscopy and xeroradiography and any testing or calibrating of such plant;

(b) any use of a radiation generator or sealed source equipment for irradiation purposes including disinfestation, sterilisation and induction of changes in the matter being irradiated, also any testing, calibrating or research carried out with or by such plant;

(c) any trial use and testing of radiation generators, sealed source equipment and machines which generate ionising radiation incidentally, when this is carried out at the place of manufacture or repair. Use and testing of such plant at its place of use is dealt with in Section 8 of this Part of the Code; and

(d) the loading and unloading of sealed sources in or from any of the above sealed source equipment;

but *not* to the following processes:

(e) the use of sealed source equipment of activity such that, at a distance of 1 m through air, it is incapable of giving an instantaneous dose rate greater than $1\,\text{mSvh}^{-1}$;

(f) the testing of gauging equipment primarily used for measurements on persons and animals (such as bone mineralisation analysers) in places other than where they are intended to be used. Testing in the normal place of use is covered by Section 3 of this Part of the Code;

(g) the manipulation of radioactive targets for machines, and the protection against induced radioactivity associated with the use of machines;

(h) the use of ionising radiation from a nuclear reactor in any of the processes listed above;

(i) site radiography (this is covered in Section 7 of this Part of the Code); or

(j) medical exposures.

Segregation and enclosure

41 The work with ionising radiations should be carried out inside a walled enclosure or cabinet and no other work involving persons should take place in the enclosure (or cabinet) except when the process involving ionising radiation has been completed or terminated.

Shielding

42 The enclosure or cabinet should provide adequate shielding (see paragraph 13 in Part 1 of this Code). In determining whether adequate shielding has been provided at open-top enclosures account will need to be taken of scattered radiation from above the enclosure (sky-shine).

Exclusion of persons

43 Persons should be effectively excluded from the enclosure (or cabinet) when the work involving ionising radiation is under way. When this cannot be avoided for the purpose of commencing or terminating an exposure, then a person entering should not be exposed to an instantaneous dose rate exceeding $2\,\text{mSvh}^{-1}$.

The doses of ionising radiation received by such persons should be kept as low as reasonably practicable by means of appropriate use of local shielding, control of the useful beam size, direction and duration, and appropriate selection of source strength of any sealed source used. In such cases no more than one useful beam should be emitting at the same time and any changes in the set-up inside the enclosure must not involve persons being inside when the work is under way.

Access should never be permitted into an enclosure or cabinet during the exposure:

(a) when a radiation generator is used; or

(b) in the case of sealed source equipment, when the source is one of sufficient activity to give an instantaneous dose rate during exposure greater than $10\,\text{mSvmin}^{-1}$ at any point 1 m from the source.

Warning signals

44 Effective warning should be given to all persons in the vicinity of the work, including persons who may be inside, by means of clear and unambiguous visible and/or audible signals:

(a) when a useful beam is about to be emitted; and

(b) whilst a useful beam is being emitted from a radiation generator or sealed source.

The advance warning signal in (a) and the warning signal in (b) should be readily distinguishable from each other. This provision should be observed in all cases, except that when the process is inside a closed cabinet of total enclosed volume of less than $0.2\,\text{m}^3$ of free space, the advance warning signal may be dispensed with.

45 The signals should be arranged to operate automatically for all radiation generators and for any sealed source equipment where the instantaneous dose rate exceeds $10\,\text{mSvmin}^{-1}$ at 1 m from the source.

Notices

46 Notices that make clear to all persons approaching any opening in an enclosure (or cabinet) the significance of the enclosure and warning signals should be provided and displayed.

Effective devices

47 Effective devices should be provided and maintained so that:

(a) it is not possible to expose a useful beam while any door or similar access to an enclosure (or cabinet) is open;

(b) exposure of a useful beam ceases if the door is opened; and

(c) exposure of a useful beam in an enclosure does not commence on the mere act of closing a door.

These devices should be designed and installed in such a manner that if they fail to operate no exposure of persons can occur.

48 It may not always be possible with sealed source equipment to provide such effective devices because of the method of controlling the source. Where the instantaneous dose rate at 1 m from the source exceeds $10\,\text{mSvmin}^{-1}$ then a method of controlling the source should be provided that allows the requirements of paragraph 47 to be met.

Alarms

49 For the protection of persons who may, despite precautions, be shut inside the room or enclosure, an alarm should be provided and one or more of the following:

(a) the means of exit should be so positioned, constructed and maintained that those persons can leave the room or enclosure without delay and without passing through the useful beam;

(b) means should be provided and maintained whereby those persons can quickly control all the sources of ionising radiation within the room or enclosure without passing through the useful beam; or

(c) where it is not practicable for persons to leave the enclosure, shielding to reduce the instantaneous dose rate to less than $7.5\,\mu\text{Svh}^{-1}$ should be provided for those persons within the room or enclosure.

50 Where the instantaneous dose rate exceeds $50\,\mathrm{mSvmin^{-1}}$ at 1 m from the source of ionising radiation a search and lock-up system (see paragraph 19(e) of Part 1) should be provided and maintained to ensure that no one has been accidentally shut inside at the beginning of an exposure.

Location of control points

51 Control points for all radiation generators and for sealed source equipment where the instantaneous dose rate exceeds $10\,\mathrm{mSvmin^{-1}}$ at 1 m from the source should be outside the enclosure. Other sealed source equipment should have the control point outside where reasonably practicable but in any case the instantaneous dose rate at the control point should not exceed $2\,\mathrm{mSvh^{-1}}$.

Other operational precautions

52 After each exposure using sealed source equipment a check should be made using monitoring equipment to ensure that the source has retracted properly into its shield or container.

53 All sealed sources should be moved by remote control or, when this is not reasonably practicable, by using a handling tool or apparatus. Whenever sealed sources are moved in this way particular care should be taken to ensure that no part of the body can come into close proximity to an inadequately shielded source.

54 Fluoroscopy devices should be provided with means of viewing which do not permit direct vision of the fluoroscopy screen.

Exposure containers

55 Every exposure container used in connection with radiography should comply so far as is reasonably practicable with British Standard BS 5650: 1978. The position of the shutter on an exposure container should be clearly indicated (i.e. open or shut). Every exposure container should have a lock to prevent unintended or unauthorised exposure. The lock should be so arranged that if it becomes defective it will not prevent retraction of a source and the act of unlocking should not give rise to immediate exposure of a source. The keys for the locks on exposure containers should be kept secure at all times, and should be made available only to authorised persons.

Loading and unloading sealed sources in and from sealed source equipment

56 The precautions listed in paragraphs 41 to 55 should always be followed where possible. If a particular safeguard cannot be used then the work should be carried out under a permit to work (see paragraph 21 of Part 1) that specifies the method of working to keep doses as low as reasonably practicable. Such permits should involve consultation with the radiation protection adviser and the work should be supervised to ensure that the correct procedure is followed.

SECTION 7
Site radiography

Scope

57 This section applies in circumstances where it is not reasonably practicable to carry out radiography in an enclosure or cabinet that complies with Regulation 6(2) and is as described in Section 6 of this Part of the Code. It also applies to radiography carried out under water.

Segregation of work

58 The controlled area within which the radiography takes place should be segregated by means of a barrier at such a position that the instantaneous dose rate due to radiography work does not exceed $7.5\,\mu\mathrm{Svh^{-1}}$ outside it. The purpose of the barrier is to prevent access by other than classified persons associated with the radiography work. No other work involving persons should take place within the area marked off by barriers while radiography is being done. Where the work is carried out by divers under water and no other persons are in the vicinity during radiography exposures, barriers may be neither feasible nor necessary; delineation may then consist of a written description, which should be conveniently accessible to the divers involved, of the extent of the controlled area.

Shielding

59 Where local shielding of sources would reduce the size of the controlled area (which may also further restrict exposure) then such shielding, which includes collimation, should be used.

Exclusion of persons

60 In general no person should be within the controlled area during the radiographic exposure. Where this cannot be avoided for the purpose of commencing or terminating an exposure, a person entering should not be exposed to an instantaneous dose rate in excess of $2\,\text{mSvh}^{-1}$.

Warning signals

61 Warning signals, which may be audible or visible or both, should be clear, unambiguous, and carefully situated so that any person within or approaching the controlled area is made aware of the impending or actual presence of radiation.

62 This means that two warnings should be given, the first immediately prior to, and the second during, the radiography exposure. There should be a difference and a clear distinction between these two warnings. For work underwater, except when paragraph 63 applies, the verbal instruction by the diver for exposure to commence can be taken to be the warning signal immediately prior to exposure provided that all persons in the vicinity are operating the same intercommunication system.

63 For all X-ray equipment, or for sealed source equipment where the instantaneous dose rate is greater than $10\,\text{mSvmin}^{-1}$ at 1 m from the source, the warning signals should operate automatically and be connected such that if the signals do not operate the exposure cannot be started.

Notices

64 Notices should explain the significance of the barrier and the meaning of the warning signals to all persons approaching the boundary of the controlled area.

Location of the control point

65 The control point for the equipment should be outside the controlled area; where this is not reasonably practicable the provisions in paragraph 60 should be followed.

Other operational requirements

66 Once the exposure has commenced no alterations should be made to the radiographic set-up until the exposure has been terminated.

67 After every exposure using sealed source equipment, a check using a monitoring instrument should be made to ensure that the source has retracted properly into its shield or container. A handling tool or some means of remote control should be used when a sealed source needs to be moved from its containment. Particular care should be exercised with hand extraction source containers.

68 X-ray equipment should be provided with effective means of isolation that prevent unauthorised use, e.g. locking-off arrangements.

Exposure containers

69 Every exposure container used in connection with radiography should comply so far as is reasonably practicable with British Standard BS 5650: 1978.

70 The position of the shutter on an exposure container should be clearly indicated (i.e. open or shut).

71 Every exposure container should have a lock to prevent unintended or unauthorised exposure. The lock should be so arranged that if it become defective it will not prevent retraction of a source and the act of unlocking should not give rise to immediate exposure of a source. The keys for the locks on exposure containers should be kept secure at all times and should be made available only to authorised persons.

SECTION 8
Use of gauging and detection devices and sources of incidental ionising radiation

Scope

72 This section of the Code applies to the following processes:

(a) any use and testing of equipment containing radioactive substances or radiation generators for thickness gauging, level gauging, density gauging and other analytical inspection or gauging purposes except in such cases where the equipment is primarily used for measurements on human beings or animals;

(b) any use and testing of static eliminators and smoke detectors where these incorporate one or more radioactive sources;

(c) any use and testing of any equipment which generates ionising radiation incidentally, including electron beam welding apparatus, electron microscopes, radar equipment and thermionic valves, when they are at their normal place of use. (When they are being used or tested ancillary to the process of manufacture or repair at a place other than where they are normally used, Section 6 of this Part of the Code applies); and

(d) the loading or unloading of radioactive sources in or from any of the above equipment containing radioactive sources.

Provisions relating to the processes in paragraph 72(a), (b) and (d)

Segregation of the work

73 Restriction of exposure should be met by enclosing and shielding any beam of ionising radiation produced by the equipment and by preventing access by parts of the body to any beams of ionising radiation within the equipment, by using the methods described in paragraphs 74 to 76.

74 The equipment should be provided with adequate shielding (see paragraph 13 of Part 1 of this Code). The shielding may form part of the equipment, be added to it, or be provided by accessories used with the equipment.

75 Access into any beam or field of ionising radiation inside the equipment should be prevented. There are several ways of achieving this: they include the permanent structure of the equipment, additions to the structure, a screen or a photoelectric system.

Effective devices

76 To ensure that the barriers and shielding give the required standard of protection, further safety features should be provided where part of the equipment can readily be moved to allow emergence of or access to a beam or field of radiation. These effective devices should, in the case of a radiation generator, automatically de-energise it and in the case of a radioactive substance should either retract the source or close some form of shutter mechanism so as to shield the beam or field of ionising radiation.

Automatic signals for radiation generators

77 All persons in the immediate vicinity should be given warning when a radiation generator is in a state of readiness to emit ionising radiation and when it is emitting. Such warning should be given by means of clear and unambiguous visible or audible signals. These warning signals should operate automatically.

Signals and marking of source containers

78 The equipment containing radioactive substances should be clearly and durably marked to indicate that it contains radioactive material; effective visible or audible signals should indicate whether any shutter is open or shut or a cover or shield removed.

Provisions relating to the processes covered by paragraph 72(c)

79 Equipment which generates ionising radiation incidentally should be provided with adequate shielding (see paragraph 13 of Part 1).

Effective devices

80   Where access to the inside of the equipment is required for any purpose, and the dose rate inside the equipment is such that it is reasonably foreseeable that persons working there or inserting parts of their body therein would otherwise receive an overexposure, effective devices should be provided which terminate the emission of ionising radiation when any access panel or door is opened. Such devices should be designed and installed to fail to safety.

81   Equipment which gives rise to an instantaneous dose rate greater than $2.5\,\mu Svh^{-1}$ at or near the surface should be identified and labelled or marked on the outside (e.g. on any cabinet) with a warning sign indicating a risk of ionising radiation. Where access to the inside of any equipment is possible, individual sources of incidental ionising radiation within it should be clearly and separately labelled or marked with a warning sign. These warning signs should comply with the Safety Signs Regulations 1980 (SI No. 1471) and with British Standards BS 3510: 1968 and BS 5378: 1980.

SECTION 9
X-ray optics

Scope

82   This section of the Code applies to any use or testing of a radiation generator for X-ray optics including crystallography, diffraction, emission and absorption spectrometry.

Segregation of the work

83   Dose restriction should be achieved by segregating equipment from persons either by:

(a) the provision of an enclosure, which may be a room or a purpose-made structure, or a photoelectric system the interruption of which stops the emission of ionising radiations; or

(b) the provision of a close fitting enclosure of the beam and covers for any openings in the equipment through which X-rays could emerge.

Shielding

84   The material used for segregation should be capable of providing adequate shielding from the residual radiation from the useful beam and against scattered radiation (see paragraph 13 of Part 1). In many cases the shielding will form part of the equipment, i.e. covers, backstops, collimators, shutters, etc. These or similar provisions would need to be incorporated if photoelectric systems are used for segregation unless a sufficient distance can be used to provide the protection.

Effective devices

85   The shielding or barriers should be fitted with effective devices to ensure that a useful beam is not produced unless the shielding or barriers are in position. The device should also operate to terminate a useful beam whenever any cover or accessory is removed from an X-ray tube or any barrier moved. Such devices may be either electrical or mechanical.

Automatic indications

86   All persons in the immediate vicinity of the equipment should know when an X-ray tube is in a state of readiness to emit X-rays; automatic means of indicating this should be provided. Where a shutter is provided its position should be clearly indicated; the indicator should operate automatically where reasonably practicable.

87   Exceptionally it may be necessary to obtain access into the enclosure whilst the X-ray tube is energised and a shutter is open. An example would be where it is not practicable to use a recognised technique with all the safety features in place and it is not reasonably practicable to provide alternative safety features which could be used with the chosen technique.

88 In those cases covered by paragraph 87, where instantaneous dose rates in the beam averaged over 1 cm² exceed $2.0\,\text{mSvh}^{-1}$ and where exposure to the beam is reasonably foreseeable, a permit to work system (see paragraph 21 of Part 1) should be instituted and followed. The system should specify precisely how the work should be undertaken and under what conditions, e.g. what safety features are to be retained. Such systems should be supervised to ensure that the work is being done as specified. Only a named person should have access to any facility provided to override the devices, which should be restored to normal operation as soon as the particular operation has been completed, or where the permit to work has expired or has been cancelled.

89 Where paragraph 87 applies and dose rates are so low, or exposure to the beam is so improbable, that an overexposure is most unlikely to occur the employer may, in place of a permit to work, draw up a method of conducting the work that keeps doses to persons as low as reasonably practicable and which should be included in the local rules. Supervision should be exercised to ensure that the method set down is followed.

Appendix

Health and Safety Executive
Ionising Radiations Regulations 1985

Notification of initial intention to work with ionising radiation or of significant changes in its use

Notes

1. Under Regulations 5(2), 5(6) and Schedule 4 of the Ionising Radiations Regulations 1985 notification is required when an employer commences work with ionising radiation for the first time. Exemptions to this requirement are contained in Schedule 3 of the Regulations which is reproduced overleaf.

2. Employers who undertake work with ionising radiation at premises other than their own will only need to notify that they are in that business and will not need to notify each subsequent address at which they do their work. However an exception to this would be where additional particulars are required by the Health and Safety Executive.

3. Space is provided at 6 for the convenience of any employer who occupies several premises operating under the same name.

---

1. Name and address of employer

                                                                    Postcode

2. Address of premises where, or from where, the work is to be carried on

                                                                    Postcode

3. Nature of business

4. Do you intend to use

a) sealed sources   Yes ☐   No ☐

b) unsealed radioactive substances   Yes ☐   No ☐

c) a radiation generator   Yes ☐   No ☐

or

d) is the notification the result of exposure to the
    short lived daughters of radon 222? Yes ☐   No ☐

5. Mobile sources

a) Is any work with ionising radiation involving
    any of the sources specified in 4 a),b)or c) Yes ☐   No ☐
    carried on at any address other than the
    address shown in 2?

b) If 'YES', state for what purpose.

6. Multiple site employer

If the employer occupies premises other than those given above, completing this section will avoid the need to send a duplicate notification. Enter the details as shown at 4 & 5 against each address. Further details may be included on a separate sheet if necessary.

Address
i)   4 a) Yes ☐   No ☐
                                   b) Yes ☐   No ☐
                                   c) Yes ☐   No ☐
                                   d) Yes ☐   No ☐
                                5 a) Yes ☐   No ☐
                                   b)

ii)   4 a) Yes ☐   No ☐
                                   b) Yes ☐   No ☐
                                   c) Yes ☐   No ☐
                                   d) Yes ☐   No ☐
                                5 a) Yes ☐   No ☐
                                   b)

F2522 (9/85)   *continued overleaf*

Address

iii)

	4 a) Yes ☐	No ☐
	b) Yes ☐	No ☐
	c) Yes ☐	No ☐
	d) Yes ☐	No ☐
	5 a) Yes ☐	No ☐
	b)	

iv)

	4 a) Yes ☐	No ☐
	b) Yes ☐	No ☐
	c) Yes ☐	No ☐
	d) Yes ☐	No ☐
	5 a) Yes ☐	No ☐
	b)	

7.   Anticipated commencement date of work with ionising radiations.

8.   Is this a new notification or a significant change in use? (state which)

Signature   Date

Name   Telephone no.

The completed form should be returned to

The Health and Safety Executive

or, in the case of work offshore, to

Dept of Energy (PED)
Thames House South
Millbank
London SW1P 4QJ

Ionising Radiations Regulations 1985 — Schedule 3

Work not required to be notified under Regulation 5 (2)

Work with ionising radiation shall not be required to be notified in accordance with Regulation 5(2) when the only such work being carried out is in one or more of the following categories –

a)   no radioactive substance having an activity concentration of more than 100 Bqg^{-1} is involved;

b)   the quantity of radioactive substance does not exceed the quantity specified in column 2 of Schedule 2;

c)   timepieces and instruments containing or bearing radioluminescent paint are kept or used where effective means are taken to prevent contact with or leakage of any radioactive substance;

d)   articles containing or bearing radioluminescent paint are manufactured or repaired and where the only liquid radioluminescent paints, (if any) at the premises where the work is carried on are paints containing less than the following quantities of the following radionuclides:-

   (a) 2 GBq of tritium; or

   (b) 100 MBq of promethium 147;

e)   gas mantles containing compounds of thorium are stored or used;

f)   a radiation generator is operated or used which does not under normal operating conditions cause a dose rate of more than $1\mu Svh^{-1}$ at a distance of 100mm from any accessible surface and is of a type approved by the Health and Safety Executive for the purposes of this sub-paragraph;

g)   an apparatus containing a radioactive substance is involved which does not under normal operating conditions, cause a dose rate of more than $1\mu Svh^{-1}$ at a distance of 100mm from any accessible surface and is of a type approved by the Health and Safety Executive for the purposes of this sub-paragraph;

h)   the work involves the care of a person to whom a radioactive medicinal product, (within the meaning of the Medicines (Administration of Radioactive Substances) Regulations 1978 (SI 1978/1006)) has been administered; or

i)   the work is carried out on a ship, aircraft, hovercraft or hydrofoil by members of its crew.